FAMILY RULES

FAMILY RULES

Helping Stepfamilies
and Single Parents
Build Happy Homes

Jeanette Lofas, C.S.W.

KENSINGTON BOOKS
http:www.kensingtonbooks.com

To my stepfamily and my clients, who have taught me about the necessity of Family Rules. With special gratitude to Donna Khurti, Simi Horowitz, Tracy Bernstein and Dr. Barry Miller, whose gracious assistance "made it all easier."

KENSINGTON BOOKS are published by

Kensington Publishing Corp.
850 Third Avenue
New York, NY 10022

ISBN 1-57566-352-X

First Kensington Trade Paperback Printing: November, 1998
10 9 8 7 6 5 4 3 2 1

Printed in the United States of America

Table of Contents

Preface

I was a young adult of the 1960s. I believed in the adage "Do your own thing. Throw it out and move on if it doesn't work." This point of view applied even to my husband, the father of my four-year-old son. I was bored, so I divorced him. I cannot say with certainty that the marriage would have lasted today, but knowing what I know now, I would at least have sought counseling and tried harder to make our family work. I know now that a marriage and family must not be so easily dissolved. But in 1967, as a product of my culture, I felt I could make it alone and have more fun. I also thought I could easily raise my son on my own.

In the three decades since then, I have come to oppose my earlier beliefs. Many people would view me as a conservative, and indeed I am regarding the family. The hard truth is that many of the tenets of the 1960s have not worked or have required too great a sacrifice. Families have paid a steep price, as shown by the divorce rate for first marriages and remarriages.

The family is where the child is formed. Our children deserve our renewed attention. We at the Stepfamily Foundation focus all our efforts on what we call "Family 2000"—divorced moms, visiting dads, and recoupled stepfamilies (where only one parent is the biological parent). We have found that information about how Family 2000 operates is desperately needed. We have also found that, by teaching Family 2000 parents a number of basic rules we can help them greatly reduce stress levels in their new family units.

Most family members living in today's Family 2000 don't play their appropriate roles in the household for one simple and powerful reason: they don't know what those roles are.

The original family is dismembered by divorce. So, too are, the roles of its various members. Fathers become friends, mothers confidants and children pals. The children of divorce are often the pawns and at the same time the prizes in the ongoing hostilities between their divorced parents. The partners of these parents do either too much or too little.

The woman with "step" in front of her name, for instance, can feel left out, used, not important and not respected. She may feel that she's living with an emotional sword of Damocles hanging over her head, never knowing when the sword will fall, what her reaction should be, or what response it will bring from her partner and his children. In the absence of predictable, traditional patterns of "famliy" behavior, not knowing one's role or what is likely to happen at any given moment can—and, of course, often does—create stress and desperate times of tension. (Half of you reading this may be thinking, "Oh, God, at last someone who understands!" The other half may be wondering if I'm crazy.)

Knowing your role in a biologically connected family doesn't prepare you for the role you will play as a single parent or the partner of one. There simply isn't any traditional, established behavior for Family 2000. It's like trying to play chess with the rules for checkers. Chess is more complex, of course. Each individual piece has a specific function and prescribed way of operating with different powers. Playing chess as if it were checkers spells failure. So, too, with Family 2000. The new, restructured family cannot make it using the older, simpler rules. However, there are new rules. They *can* be learned. And they *do* work.

I should say right off that I am a behaviorist and a directive therapist. That does not mean I do not sympathize with difficult feelings or that I don't look into family-of-origin issues as needed. But I look at myself as a loving, guiding parental *coach*. I tell clients what to do and how to do it based on two decades of professional experience and personal observation.

More traditional therapists are trained to focus on how people feel. They tend to believe that, by voicing feelings, you clear the air. I believe that these strategies solve little. People often leave these sesssions more miserable than when they walked in. One thing is certain: traditional therapies do not address the issues surrounding Family 2000.

Not one of all the schools of psychiatry, psychology, social work, education, and pastoral counseling offers a specialty in step relationships or Family 2000. For twenty years the Stepfamily Foundation has been urging these schools to address issues of divorced and recoupled families in their graduate programs. In vain. We are addressing them here.

Introduction

Loving, positive rules create emotional order. Emotional order allows character, strength, and love to grow.

THE HISTORY OF FAMILY RULES

Rules have existed since man hunted and woman gathered three million years ago. Rules lead to productive and predictable interaction between people. No organization, no sporting event today is run without specific rules of action.

Certainly, we can look at the family as a team. Ideally, it is a group of people striving for individual and family goals. However, in too many families today we see no team, no rules of interaction, and few specific goals.

Once, the home was a place to find refuge from the harsh world outside. The house provided safety. In it, things and events had an order. Man retreated to his home to find rest and peace from his job, whether he was a hunter or an office manager. Through his work he took care of the family, and at home, his wife took care of him. In the outside world, he was the boss. In the home, she was.

Both worlds were respected. Each was powerful and purposeful. The role of each was clear and well understood.

Today, both partners typically work outside the home. Thanks to the stress of juggling a job and family, rules for the home seem to have fallen through the cultural cracks. Indeed, for many people, home is not a place of safety, but of confusion. More disturbing is that many of them accept this as a fact of life.

Almost every parent must work today. Too few parents come home at a regular, predictable time. Working late is normal. Regular activities, meals, and time together have become sporadic. Like that lost era when one parent took care of the home while the other provided for the family financially, gone are the days of regular Sunday dinners or the celebration of Shabbat. Children often prefer being on their own or with friends instead of their parents. And what's worse, their parents like it that way, too.

Today, we see homes that are chaotic and without parental leadership. We see parents who are good managers in the office and bad managers in the home.

At the Stepfamily Foundation, we have created a positive model that works. We took what was usable in the old, addressed the dilemmas of the new, and then built a new family model. It is my experience that couples and families do not want to break up, and that most will eagerly learn what works. Eighty-four percent of the families I have treated are still together—in large part due to this teaching and counseling model.

Rules—along with predictability, leadership, respect, and love—create close, safe, and caring families. For the coming millennium, there are new rules of parenting, whether you are a couple or a single parent. By detailing the responsibilities, manners, chores, and norms that make families work, this book fills a void for all of us who are trying to raise children.

The Family Rules is written for the new majority of families, or what we call Family 2000. This is the divorced family—usually single mothers and dads whose children visit them (but occasionally the reverse), as well as their new partners—and the recoupled family—whether living together or remarried. When children from prior relationships are involved, whether they are living at home or visiting, it's a stepfamily.

Family 2000 is not the traditional family, because our research indicates that 64 percent of today's families are *nontraditional.* Still, the teachings of this book also apply to many first families, especially those in which both parents are working. Eighty percent of the time, both parents work in a Family 2000. Whether married or divorced, working parents are dramatically stressed by handling the demands of job and family. Today's family represents a different dynamic and configuration than its earlier counterpart. It must be managed differently.

NUMBERS SPEAK LOUDER THAN WORDS

As the following statistics demonstrate, we have definitely become a Family 2000 and step-relationship society:

1. The fastest growing marital-status category is *divorced persons.*
2. By the year 2000, more Americans will be living in stepfamilies than in nuclear families. (U.S. Census Bureau, 1990)
3. When we include living-together arrangements in our definition of "family," close to 50 percent of *all women,* not just mothers, will at some time live in stepfamily relationships. (Professor Larry L. Bumpass, University of Wisconsin, 1994)
4. One out of two marriages ends in divorce. (U.S. Census Bureau, 1990)
5. After a breakup, the vast majority of men and women go on to form other relationships.

6. Some 60 percent of second marriages fail. (U.S. Census Bureau, 1990)
7. Some 66 percent of remarriages and living-together arrangements end in breakup when children are actively involved. (Stepfamily Foundation, 1994)

Despite figures like these, most graduate schools of psychiatry, psychology, and social work provide *no* specific training in dealing with the particular dynamics of divorced parents, their partners, and those who have recoupled and are living in a stepfamily. Often, the methods and information appropriate to the nuclear family can be destructive if applied to the highly specific and delicate dynamics of divorced and stepfamily systems.

The Family Rules covers the five essential R's—Rules, Roles, Responsibility, Routine, and Respect. We examine the basics: meals, bedtime, after-school hours, jobs in the house, and manners. We also look at ways to enforce the rules and we examine positive and negative consequences (rewards and punishments).

This book describes how to establish your place as head of household, the new and necessary ways of good partnering, and how to teach children to be responsible family team members. It gives you the tools to avoid raising children who are disrespectful, unmanageable, defiant, and noncontributing.

In my twenty-plus years of working with families, I have found that something crucial is missing from most families, regardless of their socio-economic class, and that something is *structure*. Most families have few rules, and the few they do have are inconsistently enforced. Guidance and discipline are often erratic and unpredictable. Many homes are child dominated and in disarray; others are plainly out of control. Sometimes it is because the parents are simply neglectful. Sometimes parents mean well but are too busy to implement their good intentions. Very often, parents feel that the way to build a loving relationship with their children is to lay down few rules and try to be pals.

My clients are parents who have realized that things are not working. They have repeatedly asserted in various written evaluations how important it is to their children and to themselves to have "rules." We see a yearning to return to more traditional values and to character-building parenting. But as a culture, we no longer know how. More than any other approach, my magic bullet—Family Rules—has helped the approximately five thousand families with whom I have worked. It will help you, too.

1. Quality Parenting

At the heart of quality parenting today are special basic steps: deciding to be in charge; using time well; focusing on a positive family vision; learning the secrets of partnering; and utilizing the Family Rules. Here is the first of them:

Rule 1. Face What You're Up Against: Parenting Today Is Tough!

Happiness is not the absence of problems but the ability to deal with them.

Many things have changed since most of us were children. The essence of parenting has been affected most by two things: first, the ordeal of divorce and the confusion it causes for both adults and children; and second, the ascendance of dual-career couples and the work/family time crunch that it causes.

The children's experience in this new family situation has been altered as well. They may or may not have two loving parents, but what they don't have is someone whose primary responsibility in life is *them*. Divorce and remarriage often leave deep scars. Many children are depressed over the divorce and the loss of their original, biologically connected family. Life for them has forever changed.

DEPRESSION IN CHILDREN

Researching this since the 1970s, I have found that the most underdiagnosed and underevaluated aspect of divorce is depression in children.

Youngsters are often sad, remote, and withdrawn, even though they may be doing well in school. Symptoms of depression include sullenness, a chip-on-the-shoulder attitude, and anger. Anger is not usually thought of as evidence of depression, but it is. Kids who talk back, don't listen, and startle us with their seemingly uncalled-for outbursts are often depressed. Often, these actions and other forms of acting out are a call for attention and direction. Yet with today's time pressures, the needed attention and direction do not come, and the behavior may worsen, leaving parents and teachers bewildered and stymied.

OUR RESEARCH TELLS THE STORY

The majority of our children today are children of divorce. Our research indicates that, of the sixty million children under thirteen years old in this country, half—thirty million—live with a single parent and that parent's current significant other. Unfortunately, only 45 percent of the children of divorce (mostly those in upper and middle income families) are doing well. At least 41 percent of the children of divorce are doing poorly—underachieving; putting down their parents, others, and the world; and often feeling angry and depressed.

The biological parent faces the double dilemma of increased parenting responsibilities and less time to parent. Also, that biological parent may be conflicted over how to divide his or her precious at-home time among the demands of child, partner, and homemaking.

Indeed, divorce and work/family time conflicts have sliced and diced both the child's and the parent's sense of family. In most homes, the number of parents has been cut in half, while the responsibility for providing parental guidance and care has been doubled.

All this adds up to the need for more time-efficient and effective parenting. What's needed is a set of clear, orderly, and loving family rules. What we see all around us, however, is just the opposite.

What we see being played out is the politically correct idea that parents need to spend lots of time explaining, discussing, and reasoning with children in a democratic fashion. Look at parents today debating with their children. We see them at the supermarket, in their cars, and at home, arguing and negotiating with small children about what should be simple, basic rules. Here we have a recipe for dead-end parenting.

Rule 2. Don't Let Guilt Run the Way You Parent.

Courage is doing what you're afraid to do. There can be no courage unless you are scared.
—Eddie Rickenbacker

Today, our kids can look good, dress well, have lots of things, and appear to take up a lot of our available time. But despite appearances, there is often a shortfall in the quality of parenting our children receive.

The reason? Guilt. It frequently dominates our interactions with our kids. Parents feel they don't have enough time and aren't doing enough. Driven by this guilt, they tend to discipline less, buy more, and do for the child what the child should learn to do for himself.

TAKING CHARGE AS HEAD OF THE HOUSEHOLD

Perhaps one of the biggest manifestations of guilt is the failure to take charge. Many parents give up their position as head of the household, both emotionally and behaviorally. They have succumbed to the popular notion of democratic parenting—the belief that *everything* is open to discussion and that daily rules and responsibilities can be broken for the slightest reason. This is a typical problem and it's confusing for children.

Here's an all-too-recognizable example of this problem:

Howie, the Megawimp Father

Howard is a strikingly good-looking and successful forty-four-year-old investment banker. Daily, he wheels and deals with powerful, moneyed clients. Indeed, at work he is cock of the walk. But at home Howard, whom his kids call Howie, is a megawimp.

Howard is a divorced father with two children—Judy, a twelve-year-old, and Jason, who just turned eight. Both youngsters live with Howard's ex-wife, a woman he views as a bad-mouthing shrew unfit to be a mother. If he's lucky, he may see his children two weekends a month.

Angry, worried, and guilt-ridden, Howard is determined to be their best pal and make every visit a thrill a minute, shuttling them from theme park to mall to movie. Instead of giving them tasks, teaching them discipline and values, he showers the kids with gifts. At home he becomes their butler, maid, and cook all wrapped in one. Throughout most of these visits, Judy and Jason alternately run amuck, out-shouting each other, or sit passively on the couch, staring at the television with vacant expressions.

Like many of today's divorced men with children, Howard is part of a phenomenon known as Disneyland daddies, a new brand of fathers who feel inadequate and thus overlook many of their fathering responsibilities. The result is essentially the "unfathered child."

Rule 3. Know That Love Is Not About Things or Expensive Outings. It's About Close Talk and Being Together.

Time is more valuable than money because time is irreplaceable.

LOVE EXPRESSED THROUGH EXTERNALS

Watch out for the "do me, buy me" method of parenting. Like Howie's, it comes from guilt. We buy things for our children because we love them, we genuinely want the best for them . . . and because we feel guilty. But unless there is enough active caring by the parent, children resort to valuing themselves through things. Love gets interpreted through *externals*—what their parents buy and do for them.

When children have a real home—with trust, teaching, loving rules, and boundaries—they have less need to look to outside things to feel valued and important.

Close Talk on Visits to My Father's House

I, too, was a child of divorce. No matter how late I arrived at my father's house for a visit, he waited up. As I got older, he would open a bottle of Moselle wine for us and for an hour, we would talk about my life, his life, his ideas, and my ideas about current events and politics. This was his ritual when I visited his house.

These are the fondest memories I have of him—the late evening talks, just him and me. Sure, there were vacations and special shopping trips, but they don't inspire my thoughts of love for him as do the memories of those hours spent just talking.

Rule 4. Don't Be a "Pushover" Parent.

The thing that impresses me most about America is the way parents obey their children.

—Duke of Windsor

Pushover parents claim:

- "I have so little time to be with my kids."
- "The home is a sanctuary, a place to rest and do your own thing."
- "I'd rather do it myself! It's quicker!"
- "There's so little time to discipline."
- "No need to have them angry at me for the short time I'm with them."

These used to be the complaints of the visiting father of divorce, and even of the working single mother. Now we hear them voiced by working parents in intact families and even by nonworking parents—all the way across the spectrum of family structures.

Pushover parents can generally be divided into three modes of parenting: peer, laissez-faire, and democratic.

PEER PARENTING

In *peer parenting,* parent and child treat each other as equals, as pals. Kids interact with parents as they might with a classmate. It may be politically correct, but it is certainly emotionally *incorrect* for adults to democratize or devalue their position with their children. Parents who do so raise the status of the child and lower the status of the adult. Many adults have become peers with their children. As Robert Bly writes in his book, *The Sibling Society,* "Parent and child treat each other like equals who are competitive, vying for love and power, and siblings dissing [disrespecting] each other."

LAISSEZ-FAIRE PARENTING

Laissez-faire parenting is another popular way of parenting. Essentially, this approach stems from the belief that if we leave the child alone, he or she will figure out the best thing to do and learn on his own.

"DEMOCRATIC" PARENTING

The most widely followed approach is *democratic parenting.* Here, parents put aside the whole concept of parental hierarchy despite the fact that they have twenty to thirty years of seniority over their children and a lifetime of wisdom. Instead, in a democratic household, everything is up for discussion and debate; rules, curfews, chores, and manners are arrived at "democratically." This is rarely anything but a disaster because households are not meant to be run by children. Parents are not peers. Pushover parents say "no" but *get no results*. Instead, they get endless arguments, debates, and "reasons why." Ultimately, democratic parenting drains away time for closeness. As parent and child bicker for power, they lose their chance for intimacy and the sharing of values.

The bottom line is that parenting without leadership is deadly to a child's growth and achievement. Contrary to popular belief, it kills the child's self-esteem. Why? Because children model themselves after their parents. Their self-image is built on who the parent is and is not. If mom/dad is a wimp and lets me get what I want regardless, I disrespect them, speak to them rudely, behave badly, and finally disrespect *myself*. This is the psychological truth. The child thinks like this: "I am loved as I am taught and cared about. If they teach me nothing and let *me* be the boss, then I must be worth nothing. So I don't care about or feel good about myself."

When parents follow Family Rules, certain behaviors are allowed and others are not. Boundaries are set and are not negotiable. Children have a set bedtime, homework time, and curfews. Children don't enter their parent's bedroom at will. Children don't interrupt. These basics are not debated—they are decided on by adults. Sure, there are exceptions sometimes, but they are exceptions to the established rule. Life is full of rules, red lights, and green lights. This value is taught in the home.

Rule 5. Discipline!

For the very true beginning of wisdom is the desire of discipline; and the care of discipline is love.
—Song of Solomon

What is discipline? It doesn't mean blind obedience or punishment. Discipline means guidance. It comes from the term *disciple*. The disciple learned from the master, honored him, and wanted to be taught by him.

DISCIPLINE MEANS "I LOVE YOU."

My mother used to say—usually after she had punished me for some infraction of her rules—"The children who don't get guidance, teaching, and discipline are the children who aren't loved. I love you, so I teach you this lesson—because I care about who you will become." I didn't believe her . . . *then.*

Webster's New Collegiate Dictionary defines *discipline* as "1) instruction; 2) a subject that is taught; 3) training that corrects, molds, or perfects; 4) orderly or prescribed conduct or pattern of behavior."

Disciplining a child is all those things. As parents it is our responsibility and duty to guide our children through life. Discipline is simply a way of teaching children and ourselves to act in an orderly fashion. You, as a member of the household, are expected to act in a certain way, to do certain things, and even to abide by a family code of ethics. You discipline by establishing modes of behavior, manners, responsibilities, chores, and limits. When these standards are violated, then you must teach children the consequences.

In life, we all know the consequences: You speed; you get a speeding ticket.

My First Prom

Family rules were laid down in my mother's home from the time we could walk. I can not remember her first lesson now, but growing up, I remembered the behavior that was expected—most of the time.

When I was fifteen, I had my first real boyfriend. Mother was delighted. He went to the same church, and his family knew our family. Dave was seventeen, a senior in high school, and on his way to college. He asked me to his senior prom. Mother was especially happy because this gave her the opportunity to make me a dress. She had been a fashion designer when she was first married. In fact, we designed it together—pink tulle, spaghetti straps, and a puffy, layered skirt. Mother sewed little flowers between the layers of the tulle and worked the flowers into the design of the bodice.

I was seeing Dave every Saturday night, and more often when allowed. My curfew for Saturday was 1:00 a.m. This wasn't unreasonable. Still, I was into testing my mother. (Very adolescent.) I probably wasn't even doing this consciously. One night Dave and I sat parked in the driveway, kissing. I made sure I was ten minutes late.

Mother was waiting for me. "I told you one o'clock," she said. There will be a punishment you won't like if you do that again."

Next Saturday, I did do it again, only this time, I was fifteen minutes late. When I came into the house, she said, "You're not going to the prom with Dave." I never believed she would carry the punishment out. After all, she cared as much about the prom and the dress as I did. The next day, she said the same thing. I made her life miserable with my whining, pleading, and bargaining. She sent me to my room. I came out with more reasons why she was mean and cruel and wrong. "If you don't go back into your room, I'll call Dave's parents and tell them directly," she said. It was now two weeks from the prom. I went back into my room, only to emerge again. She picked up the phone and did what she said she'd do.

I didn't go to the prom. The dress hung in the closet. We were all sad.

I remember the rest of high school as being rather peaceful after that. No, I didn't hate my mother. In fact, I respected and loved her more. I knew it hurt her to punish me. But she had to establish her authority as my mother. And after that episode, I did not buck her rules.

2. Rules for Success as a Parent

For so much of what we do in life we have to take courses, get licensed, and be certified. Parenting and partnering are the sad exceptions. In the olden days of the 1950s (when I grew up), our parents taught us how to parent and partner. Today there are books, but few of us have time to read. And what you read may be contradictory or not applicable. In fact, do we even have the same definition for what constitutes a "successful parent?" Here is that definition.

Rule 6. Remember That Parents Must Act Like Parents. Adults Must Run the Household.

If you don't stand for something, you'll fall for anything!

WHO'S IN CHARGE HERE?

Check it out: Do you have a child-dominated household? Do children interrupt—at will? Do orders or requests have to be repeated again and again? Who is directing this movie, parent or child?

What does it mean to "run" the household? Heading up a family is like navigating a ship—there are sunny days, rough days, and days when it seems as though a war is going on. But the center must hold, the captain must be in charge and keep the calm. The captain is the steady hand of direction and makes the final decisions. Parents must run their families like good captains.

Uncle Jerry the Captain

My friend Ruth and I went out one day with my boyfriend Jerry on his forty-foot sailboat. We brought our two children Lars, four, and Graham, three.

Jerry was a big and funny guy. He loved kids and was an all-American swimmer and very serious sailor. The boys called him Uncle Jerry.

It was a beautiful day and the wind was up—a great day for a sail. As the four of us approached the boat, I called out to Uncle Jerry, who was already on board. "Permission to come on board?" I said with good sailor etiquette. Jerry came on deck and said, "Not yet," looking sternly at the boys. A bit stunned, Ruth and I stopped, as did the boys.

"Boys, come closer," he commanded. "You women, stay back." *This,* we thought, in the age of liberation? "Boys, I need a proper salute," Jerry said. He saluted them and they very seriously saluted him back.

"At ease," he said and dropped his salute. The boys followed his lead. "I am the captain of this ship. Do you understand? You will do exactly as I say on this ship. When I say, 'Sit there,' you will sit there. When I say 'Move here,' or 'Put on your life jacket,' you will do so immediately. Is that clear, mates?" The boys, still standing very straight like Uncle Jerry, said, "Yes," very seriously. "Yes, *Captain,*" Jerry corrected. "Yes, *Captain,*" the two little ones said, looking quite earnest. The man was making an impression on them.

Ruth and I could hardly contain our smiles, but we knew what Jerry was doing. He was making sure that on a big, potentially dangerous sailboat, the boys would listen to him and listen immediately—for their safety. He was in charge, and he was going to make sure those little boys moved as quickly as they might have to. We knew he always wanted to sail that boat hard and fast. He did not want to slow down to take care of kids. There was a good wind. The boat could tip well over, putting the inside deck under water on a close tack. Jerry did not want to have to cut back on his speed *or* worry about losing the boys over the side.

"Permission to come on board," Jerry finally called out. The boys scrambled on board and Jerry immediately commanded them to put on their life vests. I never heard these boys say, "Yes, Captain" or "Yes, sir" so many times. They giggled with delight as Jerry praised them and had them pull lines and steer the boat. Those boys were so proud of themselves. And Ruth and I were so grateful to and proud of Uncle Jerry.

The family is not a democracy. It is a hierarchy. In order for it to work, we need a leader: the parent, the stepparent, or the single parent. The couple or the parent must have a vision, an action plan, a system for managing the household. This includes a style of behavior agreed upon between the couple, as well as between the adult and the kids.

Rule 7. Manage Your Home with the Same Close Attention You Give Your Career.

No one on his/her deathbed ever regretted not spending more time in the office.

THE FAMILY AS A HIERARCHY

Some movies serve as good models of know-how. Remember the movie *Cheaper by the Dozen* with Clifton Webb as the father? The whole movie focused on his management techniques for his family of twelve children. Of course issues of limited time, sadness over death or divorce, and the frustrating dynamics of stepfamilies are rarely addressed in the movies or on television. But the idea of family management is dramatized and valued.

Think back to your first day on a new job. You were probably given a manual, and your boss or an experienced co-worker explained and showed you the jobs to be done. It took time to get it all down so that it became easy, but soon you knew your direction and responsibilities. After a while, it even felt good and was sometimes fun. On the job, we can enjoy the family of our work team. The same holds true for the family at home. We are all on the same team. The coaches, or bosses, direct our efforts. We learn from leaders and grow to become leaders ourselves.

CREATING A FAMILY MISSION STATEMENT

The couple or the single parent starts with a mission statement. Every good company has one. Write one for your family.

1. *All family members, including the children, write down their individual goals and their goals for the family.* Yes,

this may seem silly, and your family may balk at the idea. However, the basic family goals that were once simply understood in every church, temple, mosque, town, and village around the world now need restating. We live in a time of diminishing goals, little planning, and few positive rules for the order of things. To make families work, we need to reestablish these basics.

2. *Talk about your ideas as a group. But it's your job to make the final decision and write the mission statement* describing the goals and values the family has agreed upon.

3. *Assign tasks and responsibilities.* Decide what jobs have to be done and what responsibilities need to be assumed in order to best achieve your family's mission. For example, one of your goals might be to have a clean and orderly house. To achieve this goal, you must spell out who does what and when and how the task will be performed e.g., Tom washes dishes; Mary is responsible for dusting. We recommend that every family formalize this division of labor in a Family Rules chart that is displayed in a common area such as the kitchen. We will discuss this further in Chapter 3 and 6.)

Rule 8. Learn the New Partnering. It's the Secret Key to Success

All wars and conflicts arise out of not honoring the differences between ourselves and others.

—Rumi

It is critical for children to see good partnering at home as they grow up. Otherwise, they're likely to repeat the mistakes of their parents. Studies affirm that most adults who experienced divorce in their childhood feel the lack of a template—a working model—for a loving relationship between a man and a woman. In addition, research shows that many young women who grew up in a divorced family are incapable, or unconsciously fearful, of forming lasting relationships in their twenties. Of the young men of divorce, over one-third are "underachieving, deprecating, and often angry."

Unfortunately, providing our children with a consistent, positive partnering model is more difficult than ever before. The reasons have to do with the complex makeup of Family 2000. According to our research, partnering today is frequently undermined by confusion over role definitions, money, work, and—most damaging—issues around partnering and the discipline of children from prior marriages. Partners with children from a previous relationship (in common with high-level, dual-income partners, experience the highest rates of breakup after recoupling.

BAD-PARTNERING HABITS

Psychology professor John Gottman, of the University of Washington, and Howard Markman, of the University of Denver, are well known for their research on both marital breakup and what makes relationships succeed. In the course of their work, they have pinpointed a number of danger signals that indicate bad partnering habits. These habits, if not corrected, spell serious trouble for a relationship.

Dr. Markman lists "escalation, invalidation, negative interpretations, and withdrawal" as warning signs that a relationship is in trouble. Dr. Gottman, who asserts that he is able to predict successful and unsuccessful partnerships with a 90 percent degree of accuracy, calls *his* indicators of breakup "The Four Horsemen of the Apocalypse": criticism, contempt, defensiveness, and withdrawal. He points to the following habits as particularly damaging to a relationship:

1. *Anger.* "A dangerous emotion which should be banned from the marital repertoire," says Dr. Gottman.
2. *Negative Escalation.* Put more simply, this means responding to hostility with hostility and thus escalating, or increasing, the level of upset.
3. *Husband's refusal to accept influence from his wife.* Over time, this bad-partnering habit (not its reverse) predicts divorce with 80 percent accuracy.
4. *Harsh negative start-up when expressing a need or request.* Compare the emotional impact of charging in with, "You've been completely ignoring me lately. What's wrong with you?" to the effect produced by saying, "I've been missing you lately. I need more of you in my day."

GOOD-PARTNERING SKILLS

Good partnerships take work, says Dr. Gottman, "They are designed, sought after, fought for, and planned." Both he and Dr. Markman note the importance of a couple's ability to resolve conflicts without escalating them. The success of a relationship has much less to do with the partners' job status or educational level than it does with their ability to be positive, rather than negative, in the way they receive their partner's ideas and in the way they put their own ideas across.

Negativity has not just to do with our tone of voice we use or the words we say, but also with the way we are "present" for our partners: the way we look, or do not look, at our partners, the way we listen and are attentive to what our partners have to say.

Dr. Markman advocates "a defined structure and agreed-upon

ground rules for handling differences and conflict. He points out that "simple ground rules bring safety and allow for greater openness and less negative effect." He notes that "few people have learned how to handle such matters well." Also important is what Dr. Gottman calls "the commitment to the long haul." Both vehemently agree that "negative patterns of interaction can bring a marriage to its knees."

Bob and Tommy: Shrewd Business Partnering

Bob and Tommy were hotshot businessmen. Bob was the talkative one. He had all the buzzwords and could sell anything to anybody. He never had the numbers exactly right, and he didn't care. That's because he had Tommy. You never saw him without Tommy. Tommy didn't talk much. He was so quiet one might think he was bored. But Tommy had all the numbers, names, and data in his head. Together, Tommy and Bob could close the biggest deals. Both were brilliant—Bob as a deal-maker/salesman and Tommy as a numbers man. Neither blamed the other for his inadequacies. They made wonderful use of their respective abilities. They were a perfect partnership.

MAKING YOUR PARTNER "WRONG" DOES NOT WORK IN A PARTNERSHIP.

As partners, we need to look for the genius in each other. In a loving partnership, as in a business partnership, we should not disparage our partner. If we do, we not only make our partner wrong, we make ourselves wrong and the whole relationship wrong. Enlightened partners agree to disagree.

In male/female partnerships, we have a lot to learn about each other. It has been documented that men and women love differently. If we can learn that, we can avoid judging our partners by our own gender mode.

A MAN NEEDS TO FEEL GOOD ABOUT HIMSELF

He doesn't want to be made "better." He didn't like corrections from his mother when he was a child, and he doesn't like them now. He sees corrections, no matter how lovingly given, as accusations that he is doing something wrong. He balks. He may run. He may fight. Or he may make the change. Disapproval, however, or lack of acceptance or praise for what he has done, may turn him off from loving and even from sex. What he wants to know is that his partner accepts and loves him, complete with his hunter/warrior ways.

A WOMAN NEEDS TO FEEL CARED ABOUT

A woman needs to feel that her partner cares about her, her thoughts, the children, her concerns. She needs to feel that he understands her and respects her—the way she is. She doesn't want to feel put down for her feelings, no matter how silly he may think they are. She needs to feel safe with him and accepted for who she is, including the parts that are different from him. Will he, for example, accept the fact that she likes to shop and to talk on the phone? Does he know how important certain things are to her, such as receiving a birthday card or hearing "I love you?"

Partnering Versus Bossing

Here is how I describe partnership:

If you were the boss and flying with your employee to London for an important meeting, you might say, "We're staying at such and such hotel. I'd like to try to have a breakfast meeting as soon as we arrive. You'll need to have these papers ready."

If you were taking the same trip with a partner, or co-equal, your conversation on that airplane would be quite different. Perhaps it would go something like this: "We'll be arriving early in the morning, London time. Are you too tired for an early meeting? Should we plan on a lunch? As we discussed at the home office we'll be using these documents. Is that still your thinking?" A discussion would then follow.

The bad news about partnerships is that it takes more time to work out specifics. The good news is that, once you as a couple learn the skills necessary to partner successfully, there are fewer upsets and bad feelings. Instead, there is a more effective way to decide about new turf, new roles, and new issues that threaten recoupled or divorced families.

As co-leaders of the business operation that is your family, you also need a staff—usually a secretary, nanny, maid, cook, butler, and gardener, to keep the house running smoothly. Of these six people, how many do you have in your household? Probably none. So write down the job descriptions of those jobs you need filled and then divide up the tasks—the good, the bad, and the ugly. What skills are needed that you don't have in your partnership? How will they be dealt with? Will these skills be hired or learned?

It can be daunting when you look at all the skills needed in today's partnering, but they're necessary for the survival of the family. Partnering is not bossing. It's not "my way or the highway!" It is coming to terms with the whole fabric of a relationship, a family, and the work/life issues of our times. For more help in this process, see the Partnership Issues worksheets on pages 143 and 144 and the Time-Energy-Money chart on pages 145–147.

Rule 9. Manage Your Money. Don't Just Expect That "It Will All Work Out."

A fool and his money are soon parted.

PLANS MUST BE MADE

Did you know that in today's recoupled families, disagreements over money are the second-largest cause of breakup? (Disagreements about children and stepchildren are the *primary* cause of breakup.) Adults must carefully plan who pays for what. Don't let big resentments arise from false expectations about money. What are the financial obligations when one partner has children from a prior marriage? What will be the exact costs to this marriage? College funds, wills, and insurance policies, as well as the underlying philosophy of how money will be spent, must be worked out in advance. Also note that, as romantic as it is to put all your money in one place, comingling monies may not be wise in case one of you goes back to court with a former spouse.

PRENUPTIAL AGREEMENTS

In cases where there are children from a prior marriage, I strongly recommend prenuptial agreements—despite the initial responses I usually get:

"Oh how unromantic!"

"We love each other. This is not a problem."

"Share and share alike."

"We always worked it out before. We will now."

"We know what to expect of each other."

I have seen long-term marriages (six years and up) start to unravel over such things as college tuition for one partner's children, the purchase of a new home, saving for a new baby, and much more.

A prenuptial agreement is necessary in about one-half of the marriages I see. Widely disparate ranges in income and/or financial obligations for prior families make a prenuptial agreement a must, just to clarify all the expectations.

Prenuptial agreements are not just for financial issues, either. We do agreements that specify such things as who takes out the garbage. Of course, we cannot enforce this. However, once it is written down, couples have some clarity about how they will partner. They have discussed the details and now have a hammered-out agreement—with no surprises.

Use the Asset and Debt Statement on pages 149–154 and the Expense Information worksheets on pages 155–157 to help you plan who pays for what before it becomes a problem.

Rule 10. Don't Fight in Front of the Children.

To govern a child is to govern yourself first.

THE DIFFERENCE BETWEEN DISCUSSIONS AND ARGUMENTS

Discussions are a civil way to disagree. They model for children a way to reach a compromise, pick one solution, or agree to disagree. Discussions take place in an atmosphere of mutual respect; voices are not raised.

Arguments, on the other hand, are frequently made up of blaming, sharing, and raised voices. When adults argue, they destroy the sense of safety at home. It lessens respect for adults and, once again, diminishes the self-worth and self-respect of the child.

It has become the norm to "let it all hang out and be honest." But if you put each other down in front of your child, you are also putting down the child by indicating he is not even worth protecting from your arguments. And you are teaching him a disrespectful way of speaking. The alternative I suggest is not to present a false front of sweetness and light; on the contrary, it is an important part of your job as a parent to model a mature way of handling conflict. By honoring each other in front of your child, you value the child and demonstrate civil interaction.

ARGUMENTS ARE FRIGHTENING FOR CHILDREN

It is particularly damaging for adults to fight in front of children who have been through a divorce. It catapults them back to the times when their biological parents fought. And that fighting, as far as children are concerned, ended their family.

Fighting is frightening for all children. Spare them.

Rule 11. Time: Use It Well.

Small minds talk about things.
Medium minds talk about events.
Great minds talk about ideas.

No matter how little time you have with the children, use it well as a parent. Get rid of the old myth of "quality time." Quality time is often mistaken for giving the kids what they want, allowing arguments over trivia to escalate, and going along with the "do me, buy me" syndrome.

Parents create respect for themselves and others. Parents act as role models. Parents say "no" with love and "yes" with love. Shaming, putdowns, "dissing," as we know, are other self-esteem killers. So is withholding important instructions about life.

THE TIME YOU SPEND TOGETHER IS PRECIOUS

Show your kids that the time you spend together is too important to waste on issuing commands that may or may not get carried out. Your rules are about getting jobs and responsibilities accomplished so that you can be together and spend time as a family in a positive way.

Remember the time when parents, friends, and children would sit down and talk about politics, great ideas, religion, personal issues, and friends? Parents spoke about their values and ideas, and children had the right to respectfully disagree.

In My Father's House

In my father's house respectful discussions were always allowed, but arguments and calling someone "wrong" were not permitted. My father was an arch conservative, and I was a 1960s liberal. He liked to quote the German philosopher Nietsche and say things like, "The masses are asses and the weak deserve to die." I knew he would say that just to see if he could get me to break the rule about "discussions and no arguments" and get me, the liberal, to lose my cool. It was a game he deliberately played to teach social skills, civility (in the face of opposition), and debating skills. We took our politics seriously, but there was good-natured laughter.

When he would make his favorite statement about the masses and the weak, I would respond, "Oh, Father, you will soon be sixty years old, and perhaps you will become weak. Does that mean that you, too, deserve to die?"

And if he ever lost his cool in response to my viewpoint I would say, "A great man, a man whom I have tremendous respect for, told me that anger was a sign of weakness." Of course that "great man" was him. He turned me into a good debater; able to deal skillfully and respectfully with all the very different points of view I encountered in my job as a reporter and in life. We had many disagreements about hot topics but few arguments. Father's rule made it always safe to try out ideas and endeavor to make a winning point, and he showed his pride in us when we stated our positions well.

Rule 12. Be Aware That Television Can Be an Abused Substance.

Children learn in three simple ways: imitation, imitation, imitation.

TELEVISION'S ROLE IN OUR LIVES

Think of television as a drug. Just look at people watching it. They *look* drugged—or at least, "zoned." The same goes for video games and the Internet.

Consider these common scenarios:

1. Parents come home exhausted, sit in front of the TV, eat in front of the TV, and have most of their communication and conversation with their kids over the noise of the TV.
2. Kids go to their separate rooms, watch their TVs, and eat their separate fast-food dinners.
3. After divorce, when the child visits (usually every other weekend), the TV is on when the child arrives and/or the child is allowed to put it on. On those visiting weekends, how is most time spent? In front of the TV or watching rental movies.

Where is the family in these scenarios? In the TV?

Young minds come into this world pure in spirit, like a clean slate, which we as their parents and a society fill up with our ideas, visions, and value systems. Parents and society are responsible for what our children become. Years ago parents could rely on society to help in the delicate job of molding a young mind into a good citizen, but these days, parents must monitor what society prescribes.

In the average household the TV set is on twenty-five hours a week (nationwide statistics). And what happens to the child who sits in front of the TV this much? Worringly, many recent studies have shown that TV destroys active, proactive, and interactive brain cells.

Certainly, well-selected dramatic and educational programming is a valuable resource for the child and the family. Television is, after all, the greatest teaching medium of our times. It has an influence of unmeasurable proportions. Unfortunately, many parents let television provide all the teaching and guiding their children get.

THE POSITIVE USES OF TV

A family is gathered around the TV watching one of the *Star Wars* movies. The parents have created a festive atmosphere, complete with a set time to start, as well as popcorn and other goodies. Everyone watches together. After the movie, the family discusses just what exactly Luke Skywalker learned from his mentor, Ben (Obi-Wan) Kenobi ("Trust the Force"), or Yoda, the master teacher of all the Jedi Warriors ("Don't try—*do!*"). How did Luke change?

Or for a history class assignment on transportation, Johnny— and perhaps the whole family—watches that wonderful PBS special on the railroads. Documentaries are an acquired taste only. Twenty years ago, documentaries were regularly programmed on TV, but in today's market, violence brings the ratings. Too many children are too saturated with action and MTV to pay attention to what might be a "learning experience."

Parents need to insist that children watch good programming. Too often we hear parents saying, "My kids will not sit through that." Our job as parents is to help our children to acquire the taste, to teach them the ability to sit and learn and even become fascinated with knowledge. Learning and curiosity are values taught in the home. Of course great teachers inspire our youngsters, but parents create the desire for inspiration.

The Negative Impacts of TV

Too much television-watching diminishes a child's ability to be proactive. This means the child is less alert, takes less initiative, and becomes used to being passive, as opposed to active, in all aspects of life. Furthermore, a child's ability to listen is impaired by watching too much television. This doesn't mean that the child cannot hear. But he or she has so much aural stimulation that paying attention to what is said is difficult. It gets filtered out and becomes of less value. Auditory stimulation has to be loud and often violent to get a reaction.

TV and Learning Disabilities

Additionally, in my opinion, many of the symptoms of learning disabilities are triggered early, due to excessive television watching, which numbs brain responses.

Here are several common symptoms observed in children who watch too much television:

- "Zoning," or not being "present"
- Not hearing when spoken to
- Inability to concentrate, or to filter out unimportant noise (like an airplane passing overhead) from necessary sounds (like the teacher's voice)
- Inability to remember and complete assignments
- Inability to focus
- A tendency to hyperfocus (to focus to the exclusion of all else—total concentration) when stimulated by what they are doing

A primary symptom of Attention Deficit with Hyperactivity Disorder (ADHD) and Attention Deficit Disorder (ADD) (the fastest-growing medicated maladies among our youngsters) is the inability to pay attention. Both disorders diminish the capacity to focus, while often increasing the ability to hyperfocus. Watch any child with ADHD or ADD at a video game, and you will see a hyperfocused child. He is totally attentive and is able to screen out all else. Watch this same child in the classroom and he is "distracted . . . out the window . . . not there."

Rule 13. Interact as a Family. Play Board Games and Sports Together.

We act as though comfort and luxury were the chief requirements of life, when all that we need to make us happy is something to be enthusiastic about.

—Charles Kingsley

STRATEGIES AND TACTICS IN GAMES AND IN LIFE

Life is full of competition—winning, losing, being a good sport, and learning from mistakes, so we need to instill strategies and tactics early. But let's take the seriousness out of competition, making it mostly fun and second nature.

In my practice I have talked to hundreds of youngsters who say that they quit a team because the coach was "mean." ("He didn't let me play the position I wanted, so I quit.") Everywhere we see kids simply not responding to the drills of coaches and teachers. The reason? Parents have too little time, and they spend little of the time they do have teaching the necessary skills of listening to a coach, doing something because the authority figure said so, or just because "these are the rules of the game."

The Benefits of Playing Board Games

I ask parents and partners if they can remember playing board games or card games with family, friends or grandparents. I talk about learning the rules of Monopoly, Scrabble, checkers, and card games like Go Fish or Hearts. Even the simplest of card games teaches sorting and logic skills, fairness, rules, and most of all, social interaction. How we play games in the family teaches us the game of life. It teaches us how to utilize our strengths. It teaches compassion for younger children or those less skilled and ways to involve them in the play.

As youngsters get older, it's important to play regular games such as chess and backgammon with them. In backgammon, you can use the doubling cube and play for small amounts of money. Why? These are essentially war games, and they teach us how to win and how to lose with sportsmanship.

What About Video Games?

So what about the games found in arcades and movie houses that are now so loved by kids? I make a practice of feeding young kids quarters so I can understand these games. Certainly, I have never won. Every eight-year-old boy can beat me. Take a look at the difference between video (or arcade) games and board games. Yes, in front of the screen, kids are totally focused and paying attention, but where is the teaching? These games,—mostly about killing bad guys,—do develop manual dexterity and eye-hand coordination, both of which are important skills. But where are the social skills? What life lessons are they learning? Better to limit these to a few quarters and teach family games at home.

Games with the Men in My Family

I have had three strong brothers, a father, and a husband
who won at most games we played. So I did two things.

First, when Dad wanted to teach me chess or my pals
wanted to teach me backgammon, I used to say, "Only
if we play with you correcting me and telling me the whys
of every move until I can begin to win on my own."
Sometimes this took many, many attempts. But I learned,
and we all had fun. I find that most people like to teach.
For instance, to insure that a child doesn't make disheartening
mistakes when he is first learning, you can gently say,
"Think about that move. In my experience, this one is better.
Let me show you."

Second, I sometimes had to even the score against these
"brutes" who made up my family by changing the rules.
Today, when my son sends me a ninety-mile-an-hour serve
across the tennis court, for instance, I scream and hold
my racket up to my face. That's when it's time to say, "Wow!
I'm your mother. We'll have to invoke the Lofas 'girls'
rules' " ('kids' rules' would work as well). This means we
will level the playing field or make this game competitive
and not a slaughter. When I'm playing tennis, one-on-one
basketball, or other sports, it may be necessary to change
the rules so that we can have games that are fun for all. In
tennis, my son gives me thirty points, all the serves, and
perhaps the doubles court lines—he is that much better than
I am!

Parents, especially fathers, need to do this with kids—give
little points and advantages—until they catch up. Then there is
a seemingly short time when we can all play by the proper rules.
Finally, as we parents get older, once again we change the rules,
only this time we ask for advantages from our kids. It's the life
cycle. It's how we keep our family members interacting, not just
sitting and staring at each other—or at the TV.

3. The Basics: Setting Up Family Rules

In this information age the complex seems easy. But what about the basics? They seem to have disappeared, especially if we're talking about everyday family forms and norms, manners and ethics, duties and responsibilities.

Today, for so many reasons, we are no longer following the ways of our parents or our grandparents. This trend is not unlike the one I saw in the many immigrant families I knew growing up. In their desire to be American, they cast down their own traditions and values. A rich heritage was lost. So were sizable pieces of what "family" once meant.

Here are some basics for recreating the lost family—only this time it is Family 2000.

Rule 14. Remember That You Are a Team.

Think about the best coach you ever knew. Be that coach.

THE VALUE OF BEING A TEAM

A family is a team. And as a team, you have roles, rules, responsibilities, mutual respect, and goals. The goals of a family are to play, learn, teach, and work well together; to get the jobs done, to provide a "safe place" for all, and to keep order—emotionally, physically, and spiritually. Achieving these goals makes it possible for us to share our knowledge, joys, and sorrows.

GOOD PARENTING MEANS GOOD COACHING

Parents, head your team. Take control of your new, restructured family. All beginnings are difficult, but the time you invest pays off.

The idea behind setting up Family Rules is to create a well-running family team. All the famous sports coaches have their system for building a winning team. Some command, some inspire, and some pray together. They all get results. The team works together, gets directions, and listens to the coach. A good coach is respected by the team. Think about modeling yourself on a coach whom you admire. How does he or she operate? How does he or she get the team to work together? How does he or she earn respect and even love?

Rule 15. Give the Gift of Structure to Your Family.

*A place for everything and everything in its place—
and a place for everybody.*

What is "structure?" It is arrangement, organization, form, shape, system, and design. We spend time structuring or organizing our kitchens, our workdays, our workout schedules, and our vacations. How about spending time structuring our families?

When we know where things are supposed to be and put them there; when we know what we are supposed to do and get it done, and when we know how we are supposed to behave, we have more time to play, be close, solve problems, celebrate, and take care of each other.

EVERYBODY HAS JOBS TO DO

In a ball team, one person can't just sit there watching TV while the other guys and girls practice passing the ball around the floor. That would look—and be—foolish. Yet that's often what goes on in a family. Thanks to family fragmentation, kids have been left in the void. They have little real sense of connection with their family. The youngsters are not made to contribute to the running of the house, and so they don't. Worse, almost everyone in the household finds this perfectly normal. This lack of contribution is symptomatic of larger problems: lack of bonding, lack of caring, and narcissism. We have to bring participation back. Having jobs in the home is crucial. Responsibility and team playing are taught this way. So are staying power, handling mundane tasks with good cheer, and commitment to being part of something larger than oneself.

Parents, children, and even guests help with the running of

the home. What happened to the old rule, "If there are no servants, all help?" Too often today we see adults playing maid and butler and the kids watching TV. What's wrong with this picture?

Ski House Family 2000—Our Kids and Their Timothy

It was spring break, and five of our kids were spending their vacation back East with my husband and me. Friends of ours had lent us their ski house in New Hampshire for the week. Along with the ski house, we also got Timothy, the teenage son from a prior marriage. Timothy went to boarding school in a town not far from the ski house. So, there we were, a real stepfamily salad—my stepdaughters (my husband's four girls), my husband's stepson, (my son), and Timothy, himself a stepchild.

It was a wonderful old house with a great kitchen and lots of room. But all too soon we found out that there were no inexpensive restaurants anywhere nearby. With so many teenagers, we realized that the best thing to do was cook in. "What a great vacation," I thought. Six teenagers, one of whom was a leftover kid who skied well, but looked rather glum. The couple who lent us the house was happy, but his Timothy was not.

So I began my "German General" routine, as my husband and son call it. After all of us had taken off our ski clothes, I would stand in the middle of the big kitchen and call out commands. "Lars, shovel off the walk. Even if it's still snowing, you'll have less to do later. Judy, bring in the wood and get the fire going. Suzy, set the table. Jennifer, clean the potatoes."

When we were making good progress on our tasks and the food was cooking, I would call for a break. We would sit by the fire for a while sipping wine, eating cheese, playing games, and talking. Then, after about twenty minutes, it would be time to go back to the meal. "Wendy, come over and watch me as I do the pepper steaks. You'll be doing it easily yourself in two days. Tim, take out the ingredients for the salad and ask Lars to help you." I was all over the kitchen, checking and teaching.

When the meal was ready and everything was on the table, we would sit down to eat. There would be candles, good food, and some great conversations with the kids and my not so liberal husband.

At the end of the week, we said our goodbyes. Tim hugged me sadly. He almost had tears in his eyes and said, "Jeannette, thanks so much for all those wonderful meals you cooked." I told Tim I didn't cook any of those meals. He and all the other kids did. "Well," he said, "I never had dinners like that before." I soon realized he was not simply talking about the quality of food. "My dad and Sondra always cook together," he continued. "They say I don't need to help, so I watch TV and feel lonely. Here, we cooked and ate together. So thanks for these wonderful meals."

As much as we think that our kids don't want to help, or that we'd rather be alone with our partner and cook without the kids, the process of doing things together is important to create family. It's important to kids like Tim. It not only lightens the load, but it brings us closer.

Rule 16. Have a Vision of How You Would Like Your Family to Work and Behave Together.

Family 2000 will not evolve as the traditional family did. We must create a plan for it.

You are the director of the movie called *My Family,* but before you can start shooting the film, you must first write the script determining how you would like your family to function. Here are some of the ingredients.

ADULTS SET JOB GUIDELINES: WHAT HAS TO BE DONE, HOW IT SHOULD BE DONE AND HOW LONG IT SHOULD TAKE

Job specifications are vital and must be taught to children when they are first assigned. How do you want a bed made? So you can bounce a quarter off it or just smooth enough so that the cover is neatly pulled up and the pillow nicely arranged? How about cleaning the bathroom sink?

Dad likes to have the onions chopped into chunks. Mom likes to have them minced. That's okay. "In Mom's house, I do this. In Dad's house, I do it that way. In Grandma's house, she wants it another way," the child says. This is not a big deal. This is diversity training, early on. The child gets the idea that different adults do things, differently. Getting the "specs" clear wherever you are is fundamental in all aspects of life. In Seattle, they wear plaid shirts to work, and in New York City, they wear suits. In Spain, it's okay to be late, but in Chicago, it's not.

DETERMINING FAMILY RULES, ROLES, CHORES, AND MANNERS

Divorced parents have no obligation to do things the same way. They do have an obligation to make the rules of *their* home clear to youngsters.

Recoupled parents, watch letting your differences divide you. Different responses and notions of how things should be done are natural in stepfamily situations. Sometimes differences seem impossible to work out. Resolving those differences is what I have been doing for the past twenty years. Hang on. This can be a rough ride. The following exercise is designed to help adults find their common ground.

Instructions: Take a big writing pad and pen. Walk around

your house. In your mind's eye look at what goes on in each room. Think and write what you want and do not want. Consider what should be done by kids, visiting kids, and adults—and how you'd like it to be done. Phrase all rules and instructions positively. (For example, in this house "We put our jackets in the closet" as opposed to "We don't dump our jackets on the floor.") Remember, encouraging the do's works better than discouraging the don'ts. When you and your partner have done this, refer to the exercise called Your Vision of the Family on page 000 to help you complete your Family Rules.

Rule 17. Have Family Meetings Where You Present House Rules Positively and in Written Form.

The family that works together stays together.

Have weekly family meetings that begin and end at a regular time. Let children know there is a predictable forum where they can discuss ideas.

THE FAMILY MEETING FORMAT

The family meeting, and the first presentation of the rules for the children, is run by the biological parent. The partner and/or stepparent sits beside the biological parent. The word "we" is used.

The rules, as crafted and agreed to by the adults, are presented in writing and the youngsters are told that this is a working document. There will be changes, and their ideas will be respected and considered. Among the topics: what chores have to be done, how they will be done, and who will do them. Family manners and behavior are also discussed.

At the first meeting, children are asked to give their ideas regarding positive and negative consequences for jobs well done, poorly done, or not done (and maybe even consequences for breeches of etiquette). At following meetings, consequences are refined and family issues are discussed. Adults run the meeting. Good manners are practiced at family meetings. Everyone listens, speaks in a positive tone, and lets others finish without interruption.

The adults decide before the meeting which issues will be discussed. If a new issue arises at the meeting, it's okay to say that you'll get back to it at the next family meeting.

Kids Have a Vote, But No Veto

At family meetings, kids are encouraged to discuss what jobs they would like to do. They can suggest positive and negative consequences. But the kids' suggestions are subject to parent approval. The intent here is not necessarily to get agreement from the children, as this is not a democratic process, but to make sure that they take part and understand the rules.

Children have lots of ideas about what they want and should do in the home. Some are great ideas, and some are not so great. Sometimes kids will want to change times and days for certain chores to be done. That's fine. Kids might also exchange chores with siblings when they have a sports practice or a date. The children should work this out themselves and inform you of the change as well as write it on the chore chart. Kids do have an important voice in a family meeting, but they cannot say, "No, I won't."

Rule 18. Give Children an Allowance to Teach Them the Value of Money.

Allowances are part of responsibility training.

Children need to be taught that they must make contributions to the household in order to get their allowances. It's not a good idea to give a child money whenever he or she demands it. The end result is the child we see so often: a "buy-it-for-me," "do-it-for-me," nonachieving youngster. Allowances start at first grade and must be age-appropriate. A set amount is given to each child, each week at a set time.

EXAMPLES OF ALLOWANCES

Sam, fifteen, receives $25 per week. Sam uses his allowance for: school lunches, movies, transportation, clothes, and other things he wants to buy himself and others. Adults pay for coats, jackets, and shoes. Beth, twelve, receives $10 for the weekend when she visits. Beth receives an additional allowance at her mom's house where she and her sister reside. Sara, ten, receives $8 for the weekend when she visits.

Allowances should never be taken away. They can be held back and kept in escrow until the child does what is asked. Take away the allowance, and the parent loses leverage. Also, kids need an allowance for their daily expenses. They learn when it is held back. Get them accustomed to needing it and thereby willing to complete tasks to get it.

Let's say a chore like taking out the recyclables has not been done when allowance time comes around. The allowance may be delayed (not taken away) until the chore is done. Saturday at noon is one of my favorite times for handing out allowances.

My Allowance and the Venetian Blinds

In my teens I received a regular allowance at my mother's
house. It was given on Saturdays at twelve noon. My
allowance was never held back, but it was held up until I
finished my chores to my mother's specifications.

In those days, household help was readily available, but
my mother believed it was her job to teach me to clean
and tend to a home. My chores were relatively simple.
Usually I had to clean my room and the bathroom and
do one extra chore before I got my allowance and could go
bounding out of the house to meet my friends. Often my
friends were already waiting for me at noon.

Before I could leave the house, my German mother had
to inspect my work. I got my allowance only after her
inspection. Sometimes I made it, but lots of times I did not.
It was the venetian blinds in my bedroom that most often
snagged me. She would take a Kleenex, or even her white
handkerchief, and check. Somewhere she would find dirt
or dust. All dressed up and ready to go, I would hear,
"Jaaaaaanettee."

"My friends are waiting. I need my allowance," I would
plead, but to no avail. Upstairs I would go. She would
point out the fatal flaw and I would work over the blinds
again. No pleas of any kind worked until I did it the way
she wanted it.

"Do it right the first time," she would say smiling. "I have
to teach you how to manage a home. Who else will teach you
how to use Ajax, ammonia, and Clorox?"

"Oh, God, I'm missing the beginning of the game because
of Ajax, ammonia, and Clorox," I would think, but never
say. Revealing my thoughts could delay my allowance even
longer.

I wasn't angry—just a little miffed at her thorough
inspection. I knew she loved me and, after some delays, I

consistently passed her Teutonic inspection. However, I must admit that I have never had a venetian blind in any house that I have ever rented or owned.

I still smile looking back at those days. "I teach you because I love you," she would say. I think today how few young girls and boys are taught the basics of keeping a home . . . and of how few women even have the desire or time to teach their children how. But this is not about cleaning. It's about keeping the home a cherished and sacred space and knowing how to respect and care for it.

GIVE CHILDREN EXTRA MONEY FOR EXTRA WORK: CREATE LITTLE CAPITALISTS

Don't just reach into your pocket upon demand. That teaches kids little. There are plenty of extra jobs around the house, like washing the car or cleaning out the garage, straightening the linen closet or whitewashing the fence that can supply quick money and a feeling of self-confidence in kids.

Pay according to the quality and scope of the work. You might pay $7 for a regular carwash and $10 for one that includes cleaning the wheels and windows and vacuuming inside for instance. The extra money paid should not be so little as to discourage the work. Don't forget to keep checking on the quality of the work, especially in the beginning.

Examples of Extra Jobs for Extra Money

Thoroughly sweep out garage $12.00
Wash car, wheels, and windows, and vacuum interior. . . . .
 . . . . $10.00
Wash car (outside only) . . . . $ 7.00

Wash windows, inside and out . . . . $ 1.00 per window
Take out garbage cans . . . . $ .75 per can

I've never met anyone who didn't have plenty of jobs around the house that needed doing. Here are a few more suggestions to get you started:

Put hardware drawer or cabinet in order.
Paint or whitewash fence.
Weed garden.
Clean up basement or attic.
Put books or CDs in order.

Rule 19. Use Rewards and Punishments to Underscore the Lesson That Actions Have Consequences.

Life is full of positive and negative consequences. Teach this early.

Meet the child's accomplishment or offense with appropriate responses. Don't forget to praise or reward. A pat on the back, an "Attaboy" or "Attagirl," a special treat or outing,—all these are ways of rewarding a child with positive consequences. Negative consequences should be experienced as soon as possible, but may be delayed when you need time to decide on what is appropriate. The consequence itself doesn't have to go into effect immediately, but it should be announced as soon as possible. For example, the child who comes home thirty minutes late because he hadn't been mindful of his agreement might be told that he will be sent to bed thirty minutes earlier that night or grounded for one hour the next day.

Given my feelings about TV, my favorite small punishment for my son was to take ten minutes off the beginning of a TV show I didn't like. "You can watch *Killer Joe,* but you can't start watching it till ten minutes after it begins," I would say. You know how hard it can be to get "into" a show when you miss the beginning. I like to think it even helped him see the silliness of that show.

STOP RESCUING KIDS FROM THE CONSEQUENCES OF THEIR BEHAVIOR

Some behaviors carry their own natural consequences. For example, missing the bus, losing money, or forgetting work for school all have consequences. The problem is that too many parents try to "fix it" for the child. They drive the child to a friend's house to retrieve the schoolbooks Adam left behind, or replace the money Maria lost, and so on. Don't do it.

LET CHILDREN PARTICIPATE IN DECIDING ON CONSEQUENCES

In my practice, I ask all children over seven to list what they might choose for rewards and punishment. I find children quite thoughtful in this process, and it is a good exercise for both parent and child. Most parents are surprised that kids are often harder on themselves than we are on them. More important, when kids are part of the process and have a hand in designing their own rewards and punishments, parents get less resistance and more cooperation.

Consequences must be appropriate, consistent, and manageable for you. I often see adults punish too hard and then have to give in. They say, "You were late, so you're grounded for a week," when they can't possibly enforce it, for example.

EXAMPLES OF CONSEQUENCES FOR POSITIVE AND NEGATIVE BEHAVIOR

For Positive Behavior

A child gets all his or her work done well and ahead of the time scheduled.

Praise him or her immediately.
Offer to bake cookies later.
Play a game together.
Go to the batting cage or miniature golf together after dinner or on the weekend.
Give the child thirty extra minutes of parent-approved TV.

Note: Don't excuse your child from chores as a reward. Chores are what we all must do to be good citizens and contributors to the home.

A child who had been doing poorly in school brings home a good grade.

The goal is to praise the child and make him or her feel responsible for and good about the grade. The praising parent is implying that this

For Negative Behavior

A child speaks rudely or uses a curse word.

Don't yell or raise your voice. (Remember the old adage that anger is a sign of weakness?) Showing anger only brings you to the child's level of behavior. Be firm, stern, and parental.

Start with, "I didn't hear you . . . Excuse me . . . Please repeat that." And if the child does repeat it, say, "That gets you fifteen minutes' sitting on your bed with the door open, thinking about your language and the rules of this family. Then come down and tell me something I'd like to hear about language and manners in this house."

If, perchance, the child says, "I'm sorry," when you ask for the repeat, there may be no consequence other than, "Go over with me the rules of language and manners in success is not simply a fluke. The child did something to affect the change.

Make a fuss. Do lots of "Attaboy!" (or "Attagirl!") and "Way to go!" and also ask the child how he or she did that. Ask the child to think through what he or she has learned from doing it right.

If the child says, "Oh, I don't know," speculate. "I think you are paying more attention. The other afternoon you were really absorbed and concentrating. I think you are better at using time to learn," etc., etc.

this house. Let me hear them from you so I know we have made them clear."

Allowance time has arrived and the child has not completed his or her listed work assignments.

Allowance is held back (not taken away) until tasks are completed.

If a task is missed (if, for example, the dog hasn't been fed or the garbage and recyclables haven't been taken out), the child is denied a snack or some part of the meal. Any junk food is the first to go. Even some enjoyed part of the meal is taken away. (We aren't talking about starving your child here, but about getting him or her to take responsibility for remembering the chores and then doing them properly.)

If taking out the garbage and recyclables continues to be a problem, a consequence may be that next week these chores must be completed very well and checked by you two days in advance and again on the day the garbage truck comes. Allowance is handed over only when this is accomplished.

A child forgets something somewhere.

The child, not the parent, has to figure out a way to get it. If the parent must drive him or her, then the parent is owed some task the parent would like the child to do that is equal in time and effort to the parent's time in helping out the child.

Note: None of this is meant to be cruel. It's meant to teach responsibility and the natural consequences of our not being mindful.

Rule 20. Be Predictable and Consistent.

The greatest enemy of a child is a lack of predictability.

THE IMPACT OF INCONSISTENCY

Our research findings and those of other child experts verify this fact. If you promise to take Johnny to the fair and then don't do it, the child loses faith in you and in himself. Children often blame themselves for what happens around them, including what parents don't do. ("It's *my* fault that Daddy didn't take me to the fair.")

If you tell Johnny that there will be consequences for certain negative behavior and then only sometimes follow through, you can actually do him psychological harm. Contrary to many parents' belief that, by letting a child off they are doing him a favor, they are signaling that the child isn't even worth the attention it takes to administer a minor punishment.

Lack of predictability may cause the child to argue, get depressed, or be angry. (Remember that anger is also part of depression.) Don't give in when the child argues. What do we teach when we are inconsistent and let the child win an argument? We teach that if the youngster works hard enough at giving us reasons or excuses, he eventually gets what he wants. Admittedly, that teaches the value of persistence to the child, but it also takes authority away from you, the parent.

THE VALUE OF PREDICTABILITY

Parents need to behave predictably because we all—children of divorce especially—want to know what is expected: what pleases those around us and what doesn't. We need to know when we've hit a home run or done a good job in the coach's eyes and when we haven't. In addition, we need to learn how to do it better next time.

Rule 21. Be Aware That the Tone of Voice You Use Is Vital in Any Communication.

The message is not only in what we say, but in how we say it.

Pleading, yelling, and arguing with kids is *not* good parenting. Does a *good* coach raise his voice? Does he or she plead? Or argue? No. A *good* coach has authority and knows how to get a message across in a way that will guide the team to play its best and eventually win.

FIRMNESS VERSUS ANGER OR PLEADING

The message we communicate is not only in what we say, but how we say it. If I yell, "Where did you put the *TV Guide?*" what am I saying? That I would like to find something that has been misplaced, or that I am angry with you?

I've worked with many parents who confuse "firm" with "angry" when addressing their children. When we show anger, the child may resist and fuss. An authoritative and loving "No" for a little one, or a short but commanding, "Upstairs to brush your teeth now. Turn off the TV," for the older child, gets results without hostility.

On the flip side—and equally objectionable—I hear parents

who plead with children, and even have a singsong, whining tone to their voice. You hear them in the supermarket and at the restaurant. "Allen, you *cannot* have the Twinkies now, okay? I told you that before. Why are you asking me again? You know it will spoil your dinner and Mommy already gave you Oreo cookies . . ." Who's in charge here? Obviously, Mom is not. She's too busy pleading with Allen. She's even further encouraging his annoying behavior. The result: Allen may just have to persist a bit longer, and she'll give in.

GETTING THE TONE RIGHT

How do you learn to talk to your child in the right tone if your own parents didn't know the difference between firmness and fury? First, practice your "firm" voice and notice the different results you get. That's the biggest tip-off. Watch other parents and hear what happens. Watch movies that have authority figures. Listen, carefully, to how they sound and notice the results they get.

Why do kids watch the *Karate Kid* and *Star Wars* so much? In my opinion, it's to hear an authority figure's voice and direction. Kids want it and need it. The "it" is the predictable, wise, loving, and teaching parent.

Rule 22. Don't Forget Manners. Manners Are About Intimacy, Not Forks.

Nothing makes it easier to resist temptation than a proper upbringing, a sound set of manners—and witnesses.

MANNERS ARE ABOUT RESPECT AND KINDNESS

Manners and etiquette go back to the days of chivalry. Remember King Arthur's Court? King Arthur decided that he and his knights would sit at a round table as an expression of respect for each other. King Arthur and his knights resolved to set a standard of behavior. Knights were expected to be gallant, honorable, generous, and courteous. Valor, bravery, honesty, protecting the weak, and treating foes benevolently were valued. The ideal knight was known by his gracious courtesy and high-minded consideration, especially toward women. Chivalrous and courtly manners allowed people to get to know each other better, romance each other, and be kind to one another.

Manners are indeed about being kind and not about forks. They are about creating intimacy. Not the stuff of sex, but the stuff that makes you care for and respect someone, whether he be a parent, child, friend, or lover.

What does this have to do with today's families? Lots, because children imitate the way men and women behave with each other. The let-it-all-hang-out mode of expression has become the name of the game, and it's regrettable. Today, language is often crude, behavior seems to have little form, and rituals may have become a thing of the past.

The Swedish Dinner Party

Many years ago I had an experience that still stands out in my mind. It was the 1960s and I was newly married to a man from Sweden. He took me home to meet his family and told me that there would be a dinner party held in our honor. Hearing this, I really wasn't very excited. In Europe, the Swedes were known as having the most inflexible code of manners, and I saw them as an uptight people. Yet this first dinner, formal as it was, created the highest level of closeness with my new family that I have ever experienced in my life. Its mannerly behavior, allowed me to develop a bond with my husband's family in just a few hours.

Before the dinner party, my new in-laws carefully explained the proper way of skölling, which is a form of toasting. They showed me how to raise my glass and look directly into the eyes of the person skölling me. They taught me how to hold the glass and not to drink for as long as the person was talking. With all their instructions about proper behavior, I quietly expected to be bored by the whole event. After all, these people were complete strangers to me.

The night of the party arrived. We were supposed to be there at 8:00 p.m., but I assumed I had some leeway. I soon learned otherwise, when my father-in-law came knocking at the bathroom door to tell me we were leaving.

"But I haven't finished putting on my makeup yet," I protested. I had applied mascara to only one eye. "We are leaving *now,*" he said again, this time turning to go down the stairs and out the door. "But I'm the guest of honor!" I wailed. Nonetheless, he went down to the car and would have left without me if I hadn't gone racing out, mascara wand in hand. I nearly blinded myself trying to put mascara on my other eye in the car, and once again, silently railed against the Swedes and their rigid set of rules.

At exactly 8 P.M., we were at Aunt Ellen's house. Seventeen family members, ranging from age nine to ninety, were there to greet me. Cocktails lasted precisely half an hour; at 8:30 sharp, we were called to the dinner table.

I was overwhelmed by the elaborate table setting. There were five glasses to the right and five forks to the left of each plate. "How long will I have to sit here?" I wondered as the meal began. I felt lucky at least that one of the rules was that newlyweds were allowed to sit together, so I had my husband's coaching to guide me through what I thought would be an ordeal.

One by one, each member of the family rose and skölled me, welcoming me to the family. As part of their welcome, they told stories about the family and my husband's place in it. I learned that my new grandfather had been one of the few Swedes licensed to navigate the English Channel at full sail, and that my husband was the favorite sibling among all the small children when he was growing up. He had also been a famous soccer player. Even the children had some special stories to add.

As the meal progressed, I began to feel more and more affection for this family that had gone to such lengths to offer this ritual of welcoming me. As I listened to story after story, I was overwhelmed by feelings of closeness and warmth. I had gotten to know them in such a way that even as I think back now, decades later, a tenderness for them comes over me. The Vikings, who established these rituals long, long ago, knew a thing or two about establishing family bonds.

FAMILY DINNERS CREATE CLOSENESS

You don't need a Swedish dinner party to create closeness in your own family. Even if your schedules are hectic, or you aren't accustomed to sitting down together, you can still work out ways to bring the ritual of family dinners back into your home. Here's how to begin:

Establish a schedule of family dinners to be eaten together. This may mean once a week, on Sundays, or three times a week, every other night. The important thing is to schedule a specific time for dinner. Make it clear that everyone is expected to be there, and establish some ground rules. These should conform to your own family's needs, of course, but here are some good ones to consider:

- The television is off.
- Books, magazines, and headphones are put away.
- The answering machine is on and turned to low. (If you don't have one, buy one for this purpose. Otherwise, take the phone off the hook.)
- Family members can have guests only with the permission of the person cooking and the head of the household.
- Guests are expected to perform the same tasks as the person who invited them, unless they are honored guests like a grandmother or a boss.

EVERYDAY MANNERS

Behaviors

- Say hello, goodbye, please, and thank you.
- Be kind to one another in word and manner.
- Do little acts of kindness for one another.
- Help when someone needs assistance.
- Let others know how they can help.
- Respect one another.
- If differences get in the way, learn about them.
- Respect one another's differences.

Speaking

- Talk to each other the way you want your children to talk.
- Treat each other with respect.
- Use respectful language when talking to each other.
- Say hello, goodbye, please, and thank you.
- Allow others to finish their sentences before talking.
- Respond to adults with full sentences.
- Look others in the eye when speaking to them.
- Be on time.
- Call if you will be more than fifteen minutes late.
- Inform others when you plan to depart and return.

Greetings and Introductions

- Any good etiquette book has lots in it on this topic. But does your family own one? Most do not. I understand etiquette books are now back "in." (For the longest time they were "out.") Buy one. They help take the anxiety out of new situations.

- It is important to teach children about introductions. Otherwise, introductions can be uncomfortable, or just not done. The proper method is to present the junior person to the senior person. So if young Marvin has Sam over to study, he presents Sam saying, "Mom, this is my friend, Sam. Sam, this is my mom."

The Telephone

Families need to decide who will answer the phone and how to speak on the phone and how to call someone to the phone. (Hint: The correct answer is not to scream. Get an intercom or walk to the person.)

Parties and Visits with Friends and Relatives

When my son was little, I used to let him open the door to greet guests and show them where to hang their coats. As he got older, he passed trays, served beverages, or showed people where the bar was. He didn't have to stay at a party for long, but that time taught him how to greet and interact with adults.

Design a protocol for visiting or receiving guests. I think it's excellent social training for a child to be asked to go and shake hands with family members and friends. Only after properly greeting the adults does he get to go off and play with the other children.

Rule 23. Remember That Kids Like Rules.

Good rules equal good parenting.

In our research, young people have said time and time again how much they needed family structure and clear guidelines.

PARENTAL GUIDANCE SHOULD START YOUNG

The guidance you give your child should be age appropriate. A toddler must learn to put his toys away in the toy box before dinner or bedtime. Set boundaries early and "the terrible twos"— and indeed the rest of life—will be easier in a Family Rules home. The sooner we start letting children know, in a loving, caring way, just exactly what we expect of them and where their positions are in the hierarchy of the family, the happier, more successful, and more self-confident they will become.

So, when an eighteen-month-old child doesn't want to put her toys away, or the two-year-old begins with the classic "No" of the terrible two's, we must be clear. State the rules, such as "We take out only two toys at a time and put one back before we take out another," and be prepared to repeat them for the toddler. You need not waste precious time negotiating with him or her. If the toys are on the floor, ask the toddler to put them in the toy box so you can get ready for dinner. If the answer is "No," the simplest approach is to say firmly, "Toys go in the toy box . . . now." If there is still no movement, say, "Mommy/Daddy will help," and take their two little hands, wrap them around the toy to be put away, move with the child to the toy box and together drop the toy in the box. Often the child will then say, "I do it myself." If not, keep going and then, when the toys are picked up, you praise the child and say, "What a good job you did! Tomorrow I know you will do it all by yourself."

Rules and boundaries—what is a "yes" and what is a "no"— hold the child in a positive emotional embrace. Did you know that rules and such allegedly outmoded things as curfews give kids a sense of safety and security? Kids also like to test the rules. It's natural to test. But it's better to know what the rules are before you try to break them.

Suzie and "Oh, I Forgot"

It was summertime when fourteen-year-old Suzie and her family started seeing me for counseling. I was seeing her, her father, stepmother, and mother. The father was taking residential custody at the mother's request. As far as her mother was concerned, the child was unmanageable. Still, she had the talent and good fortune to be admitted to the New York City Performing Arts High School that September. Everybody wanted her to do well. The problem was that she had Attention Deficit Disorder and often forgot things.

Sara, Suzie's stepmother, was having nightmares and "daymares" about the child coming to live with them. According to Sara, Suzie was a drag on the household and would drive her and her husband apart because they always argued about discipline. Suzie never remembered anything, and her dad was always making excuses for her.

After a few sessions, we began to draw up the Family Rules. After we had gotten them in order, Suzie's father, with her stepmother at his side, presented them at a family meeting. Her father had been concerned that Suzie would resist and her stepmother was *sure* Suzie would resist. I asked them to be brave, and since Suzie was "sometimes forgetful," Suzie and I decided in counseling that she would have a printed copy of the rules to carry with her. I told her dad that Suzie could have as many printed copies as she wanted.

At the next session, the couple said that Suzie had copies of their Family Rules in her bookbag, in her jacket pocket, in her purse, and in her room. And, they said, she was doing beautifully—both dad and stepmom were smiling for the first time. Suzie was smiling too. For the first time in years she felt as though she was succeeding. She was improving in school and enjoying school. This was a new experience for Suzie. Indeed she liked the rules. She looked at the rules often and she did what they said. Especially helpful for Suzie was a tool I use called "The Pilot's Checklist."

Rule 24. Use the Pilot's Checklist.

Good pilots use their checklist at every takeoff.

Every pilot uses a laminated piece of paper called a Pilot's Checklist. He or she goes over it and acts on its instructions at every takeoff. Even if the pilot just landed the plane for lunch, when he or she takes off again, out comes the pilot's checklist. It has about twenty items on it that the pilot must check before takeoff.

SUZIE'S TAKEOFF LIST

- Make sure book bag is ready to go before going to bed on a school night.
- Lay out clothes and any equipment needed for gym or dance for next day on other bed.
- Set alarm.
- Hit the deck as soon as alarm goes off. (Suzie and I decided that to accommodate her active schedule, give her the proper amount of beauty and growth sleep, and enable her to wake up bright, bouncey, and ready for her day, she needs nine hours of sleep a night.
- Leave bathroom in order.
- Make bed.
- Eat breakfast and put dishes in dishwasher.
- Check temperature outside.
- Get dressed.
- Spend three minutes making sure you have all you need for school.
- Bring stuff to door.
- Leave in time to be at least five minutes early for school.

Actual pilots may not use a list when they land, but many of *us* need to. Here is Suzie's landing list:

Suzie's Landing List

In School

- Pay attention. Put your mind where your body is—all else is a waste of time.
- If bored, hear and write down important notes even if you spend some of your time looking out the window.
- Talk to teacher—you are being smart when you ask for help.
- Sit in a front row.
- Hang out with kids who are smart and can contribute directly to your success.
- Get as much homework done as you can in study hall.

At Home

- Snack
- Do your homework, and ask for help only after you have worked on a problem alone.
- Do your regular chores.

Rule 25. Learn from Your Mistakes. They Are Your Teachers.

Life is a series of results—Any result we don't like is something from which we need to learn.

We learn from our mistakes. All people make them. The wise person knows that a mistake is just that: a *miss-take*. It is something we learn *not* to do again. In a sport, we may begin by throwing the ball off its mark. That's why we practice until we get it right.

Learning from Our Mistakes as Parents

When we as parents are not getting the kind of home we want—if our children are sad, angry, or behaving badly—their actions let us know there is something we need to learn. Whether we hit a golfball badly or communicate in such a way that someone misses the point, we need to take the end result as a lesson.

The famous therapist Milton Ericksen once said, "The result of our communication is the outcome we get"—in other words, there are no mistakes in communication, only results. So we must teach our children and know ourselves that life is a series of results. Any result we don't like is something we need to learn from.

Letting Our Children Learn from Their Mistakes

The concept of a mistake as a learning experience is often lost. Let's say Taneesha forgets to bring her homework home from school. If her mother drives her back to school to retrieve the forgotten homework, or does anything else that shields Taneesha from the consequences of her actions, she teaches her daughter that she doesn't have to remember, and the lesson of responsibility remains untaught. Further, she enables the child to make the mistake again. Taneesha's mother should allow her to experience the consequences, while helping her think through steps she could take to keep from making the same mistake again. She might suggest that Taneesha create and use a Pilot's List like Suzie's, for instance.

Rule 26. Don't Encourage Excuses.

Losers have excuses. Winners just DO it.

Excuses don't work in good business and they shouldn't work in a good home. It's essential that we as parents teach children early on to take responsibility for their actions and not depend on excuses.

Have We Become a "Victim" Culture?

The concept of a mistake as a teacher is a wise one. So often we think of a mistake as a bad thing, and see ourselves as almost worthless when we make one. As a result, we make excuses. Are we a culture of excuses?

As parents, we have allowed ourselves to become victimized—yes, victimized—by our kids' reasons and "how comes" and "why I couldn't do this or that." Some pundits suggest that we have become a "victim" culture. We bond with each other over what was *done to us*. We can't be responsible because we are victims—of divorce, bad parents, too much work, etc. Therefore, we aren't responsible. We are victims. We have reasons and excuses. It's not our fault.

I hear young boys calling their coaches "unfair" because they didn't get to play the position they wanted. I hear youngsters call teachers "mean" because they received a poor grade on a paper. Worse, I have heard parents agree with the child, saying "Poor Chris. His teacher is mean. After all, he did do his homework," as opposed to finding out what the teacher wanted and how Chris failed to do it, if he did. Parents must teach that, in the classroom, the teacher is the authority.

Flo, My Three-Day Assistant

Flo was a young woman who worked for me as an assistant. Her duties included data input, greeting clients, and answering the phone. The first day she was late because the trains were late. The second day she was late because it was raining. And, the third day she was late because . . . I didn't even ask. I showed her to the door and said that we had decided that we would not increase our office staff.

Today, dismissal without explanation goes on in offices everywhere. In the past, senior workers might have been willing to explain to a younger colleague that being thirty minutes late is not acceptable in the workplace—certainly not during the first three days on the job. Now, the more experienced employer won't invest the time because he is constantly met with "reasons why" instead of a willingness to accept responsibility and learn. What I needed from Flo is indeed what all employers want to hear from a new employee: "This will not happen again."

Flo's problem—and that of her like-minded colleagues— began early, thanks to parents who did not instill the value of responsibility. The result: young people feel bad because no one cared enough to teach them how to make it, at least on a rudimentary level. *Losers are late and have excuses—winners are early and just DO IT!*

Rule 27. Do Not Abuse, and Do Not Be Abused.

Where there is no respect for the parent, there is no respect for the self of the child.

Parents Who Let Their Children Dominate Them

Today we hear and see so much about physical abuse and even, to some degree, about mental abuse—and about how such forms of abuse shame and diminish the child. What is not addressed is the growing number of parents who are mentally abused by their *children*. These are parents who feel helpless in connection with their teenage and younger children and who have no remedy for their children's confrontational behavior. Most who come to me are ashamed to tell others.

Increasingly we see children who dominate the house and behave like little tyrants in their own home. Children, not parents, control the tone and atmosphere in these cases. The kids argue— and win. They withdraw to their room or to the telephone, blast their TV or stereo, curse, use disrespectful speech, and don't comply with requests and orders. Too often, kids like these raise their voices to parents, and too often, parents do nothing. Too often, parents feel powerless.

When they first come to see me, many parents say they can't get their youngster to stop these behaviors. They have talked to the child and get no results, but they're afraid to touch the child. They are frightened of appearing abusive, especially in post-divorce situations, when a child could tell the other parent, who in turn might call the authorities.

Taking Control by ''Muscling'' the Child

What I am about to write is controversial.

I feel the fear of abuse has gotten out of hand and that it is not in the best interest of the child. Parents must be in charge, and physical maneuvering—not hitting—may be a short-term, necessary strategy.

Here is a practical method for dealing with a child who refuses to obey after a forceful but quiet verbal request: Take the child by the shoulders, walk him to his room and sit him on the bed. Say, "For fifteen minutes, sit and think about that behavior." If the child comes out of the room, or protests loudly, bring him back and add five minutes more. Keep escalating as the child protests. Strategically, you must win. If you don't, you'll have the same battle over and over again. Of course, this repeated battling is what I constantly see.

Sometimes words alone don't work. I am not for spanking a child, but I am for what I call "muscling the child" or handling the child so that he knows who is boss. No bruises, no blood, but a little pain. You must not yell or lose your temper. This technique must *never* be used in anger. Its purpose is to direct and to be in charge. This is teaching in a loving way. The good news is that, if you do it effectively, you will only have to do it a few times.

When we were acting up, my mother always said, "My hand is going to fly!" Into my late forties I still actually believed that when she said that (and she continued to say it), her hand could come off her wrist and hit us. She simply had us conditioned to stop whatever we were up to. She must have zapped me at some point when I was young, but I don't remember it.

A few of my clients refuse to comply with my request for physically moving kids around. Most do and get good results.

Rule 28. Keep Your Word.

Your word is your promise. Don't give it if you can't keep it.

Don't say you'll "try." If you say you will . . . then you will. Otherwise, don't say it. Remember Yoda, the Jedi Master in the *Star Wars* trilogy, teaching Luke, "Don't try—*do!*"

Coffee with Tante Anne

When I was a teenager, we spent every summer in Berlin, where my relatives lived. I enjoyed visits with my Tante (aunt) Anne, who was once a famous ballerina. She was elegant and beautiful.

One day she invited me alone for coffee and pastries. As was the custom, she put out wonderful coffee and beautiful pastries with whipped cream, and we talked. I admired her—the way she walked, her collection of beautiful things. Best of all, I loved hearing about stories and secrets about the family.

As I left, she asked me if I would return the following Wednesday at four. I said, "Oh yes, I will," thinking to myself that if it were a beautiful hot day I might go swimming with my friends instead. She must have seen my thoughts on my face. Her tone was pleasant but sharp.

"In this family," she said, "when we make a promise, we keep our promise. You say 'yes' to me and you mean 'yes' to me, or to anyone else in your life. Otherwise, you say nicely, 'Thank you, no, I cannot.' Do you understand that in this family we keep our word? We respect ourselves too much to break our word."

I have never forgotten her words. They were so emotionally elegant—respectful of self and others.

Rule 29. Use the Family Rules Chart.

Get it in writing!

Because rules are so important to a comfortable, well-run home, I always recommend writing up a formal list and displaying it in a prominent place. When expectations are clear, children have a lot more success meeting them. Remember to phrase the rules in positive, rather than negative, terms. You'll find the Family Rules chart beginning on page 162.

The Clark family is made up of Mary and Don Clark; Mary's fifteen-year-old son, Lee, who lives permanently in the house; and Don's children, Beth, twelve, and Emma, ten, who come every other weekend, as do many children of divorce. Here is how the Clarks formulated the rules for their home.

Family Rules for the Clark Family

Manners

- We say hello, goodbye, please, and thank you.
- We respect each other and the things in our house.
- We put things in their place and leave common areas in order.
- We respond in a positive manner when adults ask questions or ask us to do something.
- We work as a team to get jobs done.
- We answer the phone and take messages for one another.
- We let others know when we are leaving the house and when we will be back.

Activity Calendar

- We write all upcoming events on the Clark Family Calendar (e.g., the girls' days to visit, games, sleepovers, birthdays, adults' night out, and parties).
- Each person is responsible for writing down his or her own activities.

Regular Schedule and Chores

Lee's School Mornings

1. Set the alarm the night before and leave coat, book bag, sports equipment, ready to go by the door.
2. Get up. Put feet on the floor after shutting off alarm. (No using snooze alarm.)
3. Bathroom: Hang up towels after use. Make sure bathroom is in order. Keep sink clean of toothpaste, hair, etc.
4. Make bed and straighten room.
5. Breakfast: Put stuff away after use, put dishes in dishwasher, and leave area as found.
6. Leave for school.

Lee's After School Hours

1. Hang up coat, put away equipment.
2. Some R&R, depending on how much homework and what chores have to be done.

Family's Weekend Mornings

1. Lee can stay up until 11:00 p.m. on Friday and Saturday and 9:30 p.m. on Sunday, unless there is no school the next day.
   Beth can stay up until 10:00 p.m. on Friday and Saturday.
   Emma can stay up until 9:30 p.m. on Friday and Saturday.
2. Allow parents to sleep in. Entertain ourselves until they are up. If bedroom door is closed, do not disturb.
3. Bathroom: Hang up towels after use. Make sure bathroom is in order. Keep sink clean of toothpaste, hair, etc.
4. Make bed and straighten room.
5. Breakfast: At least one weekend day, make a special family breakfast of pancakes or waffles. Put stuff away after use, put dishes in dishwasher, and leave area as found.

3. Homework. If grades go down again, Mom to look at homework every day.
4. Parents call to tell kids their estimated time of arrival and what they expect kids to do before they get home.

Lee's After-School Chores

1. Empty dishwasher.
2. Feed dog.
3. Make sure room is straight before parents come home.
4. Do own sheets, towels, and laundry on Monday.
5. Dust downstairs on Wednesday.
6. Vacuum downstairs on Thursday.

Dinnertime

All participate in meal prep and cleanup.

Bedtime

1. Say goodnight to other family members.
2. Mom and Lee talk for a few

6. Planning the day: At breakfast or later during morning, roughly plan our day. Plan time for chores and activities with friends and family. All events, like practices and parties, are put on the calendar in advance.
7. Time for parents and time for kids. Some planned activities with children, some with one child, some for adults alone.
8. Parents go out on Saturday night.

Family's Weekend Chores

Dad: Check girls' weekend homework and school projects.

Lee: keeps room clean, helps with outside yardwork as needed.

Beth: keeps room clean, feeds dog, dusts and vacuums playroom with Emma, helps Dad with outside yardwork as needed.

Emma: Keeps room clean, helps Mary water plants, dusts and vacuums playroom minutes before he goes to bed.

with Beth, helps Dad with outside yardwork as needed.

Weekend Meals

1. Friday night is pizza night: *all* help.
2. Family has as many meals together as possible. All take turns doing different chores as scheduled.

4. Rituals

A ritual is, according to Webster's Collegiate Dictionary, "an established form for a ceremony . . . according to religious law or social custom," or "any formal and customarily repeated act or series of acts."

In Family 2000, we need to establish new customs out of the chaos that often accompanies the comings and goings of parents, children, stepparents, and stepsiblings. By establishing customary ways of handling meals, visits, bedtimes, and other daily events, we create a consistent pattern, a predictable procedure, that serves to anchor and give reassuring shape to the new life the family has embarked on.

Rule 30. Create Family Rituals. They Will Be Times Remembered.

A family without rituals is no family at all.

RITUALS MAKE FOR FAMILY

We all create "rituals" in our daily life. Think about arriving at the office, going to bed, or getting ready for an event. You generally have certain ritualized behaviors at these times, a sequence of steps you customarily take. Family 2000 often suffers from a loss of family customs. We need to reestablish customs and rituals because children need predictable patterns.

Rituals—and the memories and teachings they evoke—make for family. Rituals are something we look forward to. Rituals are something we remember with fondness. Children learn from family rituals.

The Brown Family—"The Good News and the Bad News"

When I was in college I knew an executive with the Ford Motor Company named Mr. Brown who was constantly away on business. More often than not, he didn't make it home for dinner. When he was home, however, he didn't want anything to get in the way of his touching base with each family member. Out of this need grew a table ritual called "The Good News and the Bad News." Mr. Brown would begin the ritual by telling everyone about something good that had occurred in his life since he'd last seen them. Then he'd relate something that *wasn't* good. For instance, the good news during one of my visits was how he'd gotten the go-ahead on plans to sell Ford cars in Germany; the bad news, he confessed, was that he hadn't handled a meeting with a union leader very well.

The conversation would then move to Mrs. Brown, who would relate her good and bad news. Each member of the family had a chance to describe what was going on in his or her life, commanding the attention and interest of everyone at the table. No one member of the family monopolized the dinner table discussions; everyone was given a turn, and each turn came in a previously established order, from oldest to youngest. When the whole family was going to eat together, the kids knew just what to expect. They would have to reflect on their lives for at least a couple of seconds before going to the table—because their dad wouldn't let them off the hook.

Nor were guests excluded from this ritual. At first, I was nervous about saying anything. But Mr. Brown insisted, so, after I told them about something good that had happened to me, I confessed that my economics professor was boring me to death, which was a big problem since I was thinking about majoring in economics. Mr. Brown observed that, in general, economics is boring, and that most economists are boring. He later got back to me with phone numbers of other economists I could speak to so that I could decide if that was what I really wanted to do.

While the Browns' bad news and good news ritual may seem too hokey or structured to some, there are some things about it that every family might want to keep in mind. Most important, the Browns' dinners were predictable. The Brown children liked this. The ritual worked particularly well for this family because there wasn't a lot of time to establish the much-needed family intimacy. The less time a family has together, the more systematized it needs to be in order not to lose precious hours to confusion.

Rule 31. Know That Family Meals Are a Basic Ritual.

Animals eat. People dine.

The family meal is the altar of the family. It is the setting for the teaching of values, ethics, and a vision of self and the world. These meals eaten together need to occur at least three to four times a week (including perhaps a weekend brunch). Because they mostly occur at home, they don't have to be expensive. Bad manners, television watching, and phone answering are all banned.

Only Mungo Eats at a Predictable Time

Maggie Hansen is an administrator in a busy metropolitan hospital. She's up early every morning and when she gets home, around 5:00 p.m., she's so hungry that she prepares dinner as soon as she walks through the door. Her husband Mark, a buyer in a major department store, is not home until at least 7:00 p.m., so she leaves some food for him in the oven while she eats alone. By the time Mark gets home, Maggie is relaxing in front of the TV, so he has dinner in the kitchen by himself, with his sales reports for company.

Their two kids, Gail, seventeen, and Thomas, fourteen, are both heavily involved in sports and often don't show up for dinner at all. When they do, Gail likes to eat in her room while talking on the phone. Thomas doesn't like what his mom watches on TV, so he puts on his headphones and blasts rap music while he eats.

The only member of the Hansen family who has an assigned time and place to eat is their dog Mungo, who always eats on the back porch after *Jeopardy.*

The scenario is all too familiar. All over the country, family members are eating at fast-food restaurants or at home alone using the TV, headphones, or newspapers as a substitute for family communication and emotional interaction. The Hansens are missing the chance to make their dinner table a family forum where they can discuss their day's problems and triumphs, give each other support and advice, plan a family vacation, or propose something new:

- "Would you pretend I wasn't your daughter if I got a nose ring?"
- "I really tried this semester but I still got a C in math. Do you think I can get a tutor?"
- "Your mom just got a great job offer in Virginia. How do you feel about moving?"

The dinner table becomes a place where everyone is free to voice opinions about family issues and where family decisions can be made. Moreover, the dinner hour doesn't have to be solely devoted to personal concerns. You and your kids can talk about what you've read in the paper or seen on television. Literature, new movies, politics—all these things can and should be talked about at your family altar—the dinner table.

It's not simply a matter of sharing opinions about the world, though that certainly is important. Conversations like this—and the context out of which they arise—are the crucible for a family's identity and philosophy. What you believe—about the president, taxes, the environment, art, music, literature—will shape what and how your children think forever. And if they don't have a chance to talk with you—free from the competing noise of the television set and the interruptions of the telephone—you are putting your most vital parental legacy at risk: the sharing of your own values and worldview. These are intangibles that only you can communicate to them and the family meal is the ideal setting.

DINNER: RECLAIMING THE FAMILY FOCAL POINT

The Seating Arrangement

Establish a seating arrangement and stick to it. Having a regular, established seating order at the table is predictable and reassuring for children. If everyone has his or her place, it banishes the emotional chaos that occurs when family members sit in different places every night.

One big mistake that many families make—especially when there is a second marriage—is that the couple sits next to each other in what we call "the honeymoon position." This arrangement, with the couple alongside each other and the kids sitting opposite, looks like a face-off. It immediately sets up a polarization of "us" and "them." Instead, the male and female heads of the household should sit at either end of the table. Usually it is the female at the food, closest to the kitchen, and the male at the head. This holds true even if you eat in the kitchen.

Remember those experiments you did in sophomore science with the metal shavings and the magnet's north and south poles? The shavings immediately formed a force field around the two poles. So it is at the table. The male and female heads of household create a strong force field of unity that includes the children. The table is not dominated by children, but, as it needs to be, by adult leaders and teachers—two parents or parent and partner.

When it is just the family at dinner, children should sit according to age and gender. The oldest girl sits to the right of the male head of household, and the oldest boy on the female head's right—unless there are babies or little ones who need help, in which case they sit on their biological parent's right.

Should this be a dating situation, the female remains at the foot of the table and puts her male guest to her right. Or if it is his table, he sits at the head and puts her to his right—both sit as guest of honor. This does not hold true when they are a couple.

There must be a consistent place where children sit when they come to the table—even when they come on visitation. Places must remain the same. We find this order enormously important at meals, no matter what.

At the Table

Here are a few "rules" that will make those ritual meals work better:

- Make the table look attractive.

- Light candles; Candlelight makes dinner feel important and focuses attention toward the center, drawing the family together.
- Encourage kids to make inexpensive seasonal center-pieces—like autumn leaves, flowers from the garden, or a bowl of fruit.
- Establish a "dress code" including: clean hands, faces, and shirts; shoes on feet, hair combed, and heads without baseball caps.
- Serve dinner at a regular time; parents need to get home from work on those designated special days.

Dinner Preparation

Use the dinner preparation as part of the ritual. Often, today's mom or dad has to come home from work and begin playing chef. This not only creates resentment occasionally, but also leaves the children untaught, learning nothing about preparing a meal.

Make your family an integral part of the food preparation, assigning everyone a specific task. Not only will you be making your own workload lighter, you will be establishing a predictable way of doing things that can be an ongoing part of family life.

Once you've established a general vision of what your family dinner should be, you're ready to begin breaking it down to individual tasks. Think of old-fashioned chores like corn husking, sewing bees and cookie bakes that fostered closeness because of the repetitive nature of the tasks being performed. People would talk and joke while they peeled the corn or made the quilts. You can recreate this feeling by sharing the repetitive, labor-intensive ritual of preparing and cleaning up after dinner.

It's very important to rotate tasks on a specific schedule. At my house we like a weekly chore schedule. This reduces boredom, cuts down on arguments about whose turn it is to do what, and allows everyone to gain ability in a variety of skills. Post the schedule for chores in the kitchen. (No excuses for not knowing what each person's responsibilities are for that week.) If children have a commitment or an outing, they switch chores with other children. Adults keep out of the problem, teaching them to take responsibility, make trades, and get the job done.

Here is a step-by-step guide to assigning and delegating dinner-making tasks:

The Sixteen Steps of a Family Meal

1. *Planning the meal and keeping a list.* Make it clear that in your household, no one may eat the last of the peanut butter and simply put the empty jar back in the cabinet. He or she has to write "peanut butter" on the list in the kitchen and throw out the jar. The list may be kept on a pad with an attached pencil in the kitchen, preferably near the refrigerator. Everyone's responsibility for updating the list makes the family team more efficient and more effective. It saves time.

   The cook decides on the week's menu and is in charge of the final shopping list. Family members may express preferences, but the final choice is always left to the cook.

2. *Shopping.* When you involve children in the skills of shopping, it is a learning and productive ritual. All too many parents leave their children home when it comes to food shopping, thus depriving them of important lessons. Take at least one child with you when you do the weekly shopping.

   Teach your kids what you know about choosing nutritious foods and selecting produce. Show them how to pick a ripe cantaloupe. Then give them the task of finding one and bringing it back to the cart. Teach them how to comparison-shop and send them out to scout and tally. I like canned Del Monte tomatoes so I'll send a youngster out to figure out the difference in price (often quite a math problem) between the generic, or house, brand and my favorite.

3. *Putting away.* Children help adults with the putting-away process. Children do not just go and watch TV after shopping. Putting away teaches kids how to sort and organize and allows them to know where things are so that they can find them for themselves, saving adults time down the road. Unloading bags, organizing the contents, then putting things where they belong teach basic prioritizing skills.

4. *Pickup shopping.* When you run out of orange juice or milk, send the eleven-year-old on her bike to get these small items and bring back the change. This teaches responsibility, social skills, what things cost, and much more, early on.

5. *Setting the table.* Teach children the way you expect the table to be set for breakfast, lunch, dinner, and special occasions. If you are unsure about the proper way to do this, consult an etiquette book. To help young children, you can set one place and let them follow your example with the other settings. Not only does this give children a reassuring sense of how things are supposed to be, it also accustoms them to following instructions.

Candles, flowers, and other embellishment adorn and sanctify the experience of eating, sharing, and being together. Encourage kids to make their own centerpieces.

This is the responsibility of the table setter. Communicate the sense of the table's holiness: the dinner table is an altar of family life.

The table setter does his or her job at least fifteen minutes before the meal is scheduled to be served. If forks and knives are thrown down haphazardly when everyone is coming to the table, it undermines the sense of ritual and closeness you are trying to create. Instead, the process of setting the table must reflect the dinner that it is meant to serve: calm, ordered, and unhurried—something to enjoy and take pleasure in.

The table setter and the cook must see to it that all items for the meal are on the table and that water and milk glasses are filled. Once the female head of the household sits down, there should be no more getting up to get this or that. She and her partner see to it that all is ready.

Decide in advance if all the food will be served in bowls for passing, or whether plates will be laid with food away from the table. I think the latter procedure works best for under four people, whereas bowls or plates for passing are better when there are four or more.

6. *Assisting the cook.* This is an important teaching opportunity. Too many parents banish youngsters from the kitchen, forgetting that, as the cook, they have a wonderful power to share with their kids. The cook is the master of the meal, and all directives must emanate from him or her. The cook has knowledge, and knowledge is power: knowing when the steak is just right, or how to tell if the cake is done. Children fill the role of apprentices, or "under chefs" in this case, learning to take directions from the master—the cook. A good cook is a kind of magician, imparting wonderful skills and tricks to the

audience. Teaching something concrete like cooking only enhances the ritual and bonding aspects of your family's meals.

Explain to your assistant cook what you are doing every step of the way. First, have him watch you, then allow him to participate as much as possible, gradually turning over entire chores as he demonstrates competence. His increasing mastery will surprise you; so will his growing self-esteem, confidence, and sense of responsibility. Eventually he can take over the role of cook and you'll be the assistant.

7. *Starting the Meal and the Conversation.* To begin the meal, try saying grace. It doesn't matter whether or not you're religious; saying grace together is a bonding experience. The content is less important than the form: the idea that everyone at the table is joining together and offering thanks for their family, friendships, and the food they are about to eat. Children may initially put it down, but in the long run, they respond well to forms of ritualized behavior.

The female head of the household starts the meal itself by taking the first bite. Only then should everyone else start to eat. If someone forgets, she can say, "Let me just take a bite, so we can all start," as a reminder.

The adults begin the conversation and are in charge of the character of talk at the table. The male head of the household can begin with his good news and bad news stories, followed by his partner's, followed by the next-ranked person's (whether the oldest child or the older guest at the table). If you don't want to follow this system, just make sure your dining is not child-dominated. Adults should lead the discussions and set the tone.

Banish all emotional disturbances and distractions from the dinner table. Nothing should be said during the meal that might disrupt the digestive process. Don't use the dinner table to reprimand or belittle your kids or your partner. Fights and feuds will make your dinners ordeals rather than cherished rituals. "Why did you do so badly on your math test?" is not a good question to ask at the dinner table, although "How are things going in school?" might be.

8. *Teaching table manners.* This should be done away from the table. While manners are extremely important, the teaching of them should not be part of the family meal, except for gentle reprimands and, of course, your good example. If the meal evolves into scolding a child for the mess he has made or insisting that he eat a certain way, the whole point is lost. Teach away from the table. The biological parent should say, "I've noticed that I haven't gotten across to you how to use your napkin/when to eat with your fingers and when not to. Let's go over it now so that I can feel okay about teaching you all that I should have." It is our responsibility as parents to teach. If we don't get it across, *we are responsible.*

9. *Ending the meal.* The female head of the household also ends the dinner. Family members who must leave early ask to be excused. Kids must not expect to leave the instant they have finished their food. If someone does have to leave early—for band practice, a study date, etc.—this should be discussed and agreed upon beforehand.

10. *Clearing the table.* One or two people are assigned to clear for the week. This means platters and serving bowls

first and then dishes. Don't stack. It makes more work for the dish washing crew, and it's bad form.

It's perfectly all right for the couple (unless they are part of the clearing crew) to linger at the table with their coffee or go to another room while the children begin the cleanup. It's also okay for the family to sit and talk with the dirty dishes in front of them. Clearing plates away the moment everyone is done eating is a practice invented by restaurant owners trying to achieve high profits and table turnover rates. There is no need to interrupt good conversation to clear the table, unless of course a family member has to leave or a little one must prepare for bed.

11. *Loading the dishwasher/doing the dishes.* Washing the dishes should not be the responsibility of the cook. Let other members rotate this chore. If you don't have a dishwasher, have kids work in pairs—one to wash, another to dry. Another person can do the pots and pans.

12. *Scrubbing the pots and pans.* For this grimy chore, adults set the quality control specifications. Reward good work with praise. If a pot is a mess after the washing, give the child two more pots to clean as a consequence. Adults specify what is clean and what is not.

13. *Putting away the leftovers.* The cook comes back into play here. It is his or her responsibility to tell the others what is to be saved and what to throw away and how different things should be saved. People have all kinds of different systems for saving, from Tupperware to putting a plastic baggie over the original dish.

14. *Wiping off counter tops.* This is not about turning your

kids into slaves. This is about *teaching,* so that the way you use materials sets a standard for the child in life.

15. *Sweeping the floor.* This task teaches the value of leaving one's work space in order—a good lesson for school, work, and life.

16. *Putting out the garbage.* The last chore of the evening.

RESTAURANT BEHAVIOR

Today more and more people are working, and restaurants have become a big part of their families' lives. I hear and see many children making demands, ordering the waitress around, talking too loudly, insisting on eating *only* certain foods. Single parents—especially dads with visiting kids—are reluctant to teach and discipline.

The regular suspects are to blame: guilt, the fear of saying "no," parents trying to act like pals, and the parents' need for love in the too-short time they have with their children. Again, we as parents must teach. We care when we love enough to discipline. Children must be prepared to handle the restaurant experience: what food they may or may not order; if they may get up from the table; how they will seat themselves. That is decided by the parent or the couple. A restaurant is not a place to reprimand a child. Parents must teach these behaviors *before* they go to a restaurant.

The partner who is not the parent often gets upset with kids' eating habits and manners. The restaurant is not the time or place to inform the biological parent. This is best done when the children are away and the two of you are alone. It is vital to a relationship that you decide together what is appropriate behavior. We have all been raised differently—some with few manners, some who have forgotten their manners. To survive with kids, you need to establish mutually acceptable behaviors in restaurants and public places.

Rule 32. Make Bedtime a Predictable Routine and a Ritual.

Most children of divorce can be expected to lose sleep over it.

BEDTIME CHAOS

Among many families today bedtime is a drawn-out drama. Regular bedtimes and regular customs and rituals *before* bedtime are often nonexistent. Parents often set no regular bedtimes. Kids frequently stay up too late for their health. The result? Many kids are lacking the nourishing sleep they need, and many parents have little time alone at night.

I often see children who are kept up late on visitation nights or by parents who work. These children are essentially sleep-deprived. Any child who is difficult to get out of bed in the morning may well be sleep-deprived. When children don't get enough sleep, we see changes in their personalities. We see kids who have trouble concentrating and are often irritable. As caring parents, we need to learn the number of hours required for each age of development. For example, a four-year-old needs eleven to twelve hours sleep, a ten-year-old, ten hours sleep. These are just averages; each child is different. Get to know your child's sleep needs.

USING BEDTIME RITUALS TO CALM UNCONSCIOUS FEARS

Many children of divorce have trouble sleeping because they are fearful. Children who don't want to sleep at night and rise early in the morning often have deep-seated and unconscious fears of being alone. A child's fear of abandonment as a result of the losses suffered in divorce often manifests itself in sleep problems.

Steve, a newly divorced father, could never get his two girls, age four and six, to sleep when they visited his house. He liked the ritual I suggested as a remedy, but was reluctant to try it. When he did, however, the girls did better after just one week. At his second appointment, Steve and I refined the process even further. He and his girls are now sleeping well.

Here is the bedtime ritual I suggested:

The child brushes her teeth, gets ready for bed, and lies down. The biological parent reads a story for about ten minutes, or perhaps the child reads to the parent. Then, whether you are religious or not, you say your nighttime prayers. Sound corny? Old fashioned? It works!

The prayer I teach parents to say is one I made up for myself as a child of divorce and one I said to my child as a child of divorce. Depending on age, we may start out with The Lord's Prayer, but we end with:

> God's arms encircle me and mine and all.
> And as I sleep God's angels watch over me.
> Two at my head
> And two at my feet
> Watch over me while I sleep.

You can see why my big "tough guy" clients like Steve have trouble with this one. Try it! The process just works. I have been proposing this to parents—even atheists—for more than twenty years with great results. Children moving between homes, often with unpredictable bedtimes, can only be expected to have some trouble with sleep. Evoking God, a higher power or the Force to watch over them takes the burden off us mortal parents and enlists the help of the universe.

My Son Lars's Bedtime Ritual

When my son was between five and ten, I was a single parent and went out about three nights a week. Never did I leave the house before 8:30 p.m. This did make for some short evenings, but his bedtime ritual was very important to me, and my friends survived.

Every night, Lars would go to bed at 8:00 p.m. I would sit on the bed and read a story, and then we would say prayers until 8:15. Prayers said in a singsong way are almost trance-inducing, aiding sleep. Saying it in that way, I could get him to feel tired by the end of, "Our Father Who is in Heaven." It worked like a charm. This predictable ritual allowed Lars to fall asleep within five minutes of my leaving the room. This, of course, allowed me to go out in good conscience because Lars was sound asleep.

THE DIRTY-YOUR-PLATE MEAL

In addition to the bedtime ritual, I did something I call the "dirty-your-plate meal."

On the nights that I went out, I would have two dinners. My first dinner (the "dirty-your-plate meal") was with Lars. The real meal I ate out.

So many parents sit with their child and watch while he or she eats. Think about how uncomfortable this makes the child.

The parent is leaving, and now the same parent is sitting there watching him or her eat. It just doesn't work. This is not dinner with the child.

Participate in the dinner ritual. Spread some salad or vegetables or potatoes around your plate and sit down and eat (slowly—because you have little food) with your child. Have your regular dinner table conversations, your regular ritual meal, at the regular time. This procedure is especially important when the divorce is new and when one parent has a new partner and wants to go out.

Rule 33. Create Family Rituals for Holidays and Special Events.

Without rules and etiquette for the holidays, they can quickly become horror days.

HOLIDAYS: NEGOTIATIONS ARE IN ORDER

Holidays can be difficult in a Family 2000 because they are by nature family-centered. Rather than bringing joy, these events often seem to invite and exacerbate discord and disappointment in the new family, because they only emphasize that the family is no longer the same.

Instead of falling asleep with visions of sugarplums dancing in their heads, children in divorce and step situations may more often be kept awake by the anxiety of wondering how their holiday will go. Because of their often divided loyalties and the shuttling back and forth between parents, children and adults alike may dread holidays and special events.

Instead of blocking off the holidays and forcing the child to spend Christmas or Hanukkah at only one location, negotiation is in order. Keep in mind that the welfare of the child, and not the selfish aims of the parents or stepparents, should be most important in deciding what to do about holidays and other traditional family celebrations.

Give the child as much of everybody as you can, within reason and after careful consideration of the child's age and ability to handle all the excitement. One way of compromising would be to spend half the day here and the other half there. Perhaps, however great the sacrifice, the child should be allowed to enjoy the actual holiday in his full-time home, but spend the evening or the day after with the rest of the family.

BIRTHDAYS: KEEP THE CHILD IN MIND

Christmas, Hanukkah, Easter, Passover, and other formal holidays are not the only days of dread. Birthdays take on a new meaning in a Family 2000. Both parents and their new partners may sincerely want to help the child celebrate his birthday, but without cooperation and concern for the child, they will only succeed in making him feel anxious, guilty, and deeply angry that his day can't be simpler.

Not everybody can host the birthday party, but the parents can arrange to celebrate in a variety of ways. The parents can agree to celebrate as part of one big group in which the fighting is temporarily forgotten in the festivity. Another option is for each to host a small, separate party to which different people have been invited. (Such parties must always be arranged with adequate consideration for the stamina of the child.) The child should not be placed in the no-win situation of having to choose between Mommy's party and Daddy's party. Given that choice, the child would rather stay in his or her room and forget all about the birthday.

How to Make Holidays Happy Days

When you make the arrangements that holidays and traditional celebrations require, always consider them from the perspective of the child. Put your own concerns aside for a time. The following steps can make the difference between a wonderful special occasion for the whole family and one that leaves everybody unhappy.

- *The three rules for special events are: Plan, plan, plan.* Parents need to plan even the smallest of holidays, like Halloween. The larger the holiday, the more planning it takes. Start planning Christmas and Hanukkah in September.
- *Everyone's expectations may be different.* Stop, look, and listen to your expectations, your partner's expectations, and each child's expectations. Honor one another's feelings and concerns. Differentiate between a problem and the people involved.
- *Accept that in stepfamilies there is more movement and less peace.* This movement is endemic to the new family configuration.
- *In the beginning everything is a precedent.* Good precedent-setting now predicts a smooth future. Plan the event as though you were the director of a movie. Work out *exact* dates and hours of arrival and departure. Apply the five W's: who, what, where, when, and why. Take all contingencies into consideration.
- *Work out holiday duties in advance.* The responsibilities and contributions of each member of the new family should be thought out clearly by both parent and new partner and positively presented to the children by the biological parent.
- *The expenditure of time, energy, and money should be*

clearly defined in each family. The amount spent on gifts can become a bone of contention. People can have differing expectations about who should contribute how much energy and time. For example: Megan's stepmother has the Friday after Thanksgiving off. Her husband needs to go to the office. He may expect her, as his wife, to take care of his child, but if he wants the holidays to work, he'd better seek out her specific agreement.

- *Create an atmosphere for closeness.* Bake together, play party games, or make eggnog and popcorn by the fire. Do *not* let the TV be the only warm glow in the room.
- *Keep your sense of humor and your vision of the spirit of the holiday.* Holidays are often about forgiveness and new beginnings. For Family 2000, sometimes the saving grace is to rise above the behaviors. We can create the holidays we want, but first we must plan them.

Rule 34. Know the Rituals Surrounding Gift Giving and Thank-You's.

Find . . . the lost art of saying "Thank you!"

APPRECIATION MATTERS

Some Family 2000 children have forgotten how to say thank you. The simple thank-you note seems passé. People with manners are put off and often stop giving gifts, inviting children to special events, or doing things for kids. Generally this occurs because their parents haven't taught them how or don't know themselves. Here is where the etiquette book comes in handy.

This lack of manners is emblematic of two larger cultural problems—the lack of parenting following a divorce; and the "entitled" child who neither feels grateful nor senses any need to express appreciation.

Parents need to teach children how and when to tell others that they loved the gift, enjoyed the meal, or had a great time at the party. Letting people know that their efforts on our behalf are appreciated is just the art of returning kindness with kindness.

When the Smiths invite little Sally for a weekend at the beach, for instance, she shouldn't be sent empty-handed. (A $5-tin of Girl Scout cookies would do.) She should be reminded to help out with chores, make her bed, and say "Thank you" to the Smiths when she says "goodbye." When Sally returns, she should be reminded to write a thank-you note, and if she doesn't know how, she should be taken through the process. (At a minimum, Sally should be instructed to make a phone call to the Smiths.)

REMEMBER THE NONCUSTODIAL PARENT

Another downside of divorce is that children are often allowed to forget to give cards or gifts to members of the family on the noncustodial side. Father's Day, Mother's Day, and grandparents' birthdays all go by unrecognized by the child. People get hurt, and the whole ritual of remembering someone with a drawing, a homemade card, or some special token is lost.

A simple note or a call can make all the difference. But it must be done. This means supervising your children. Take them to the store for a birthday card or gift or have them make one. Pick up the phone and dial it for them if necessary. No matter how bad you feel about your ex, he or she is still the child's parent. When that parent goes unthanked, he or she naturally feels hurt, and the upset that may follow will affect the child.

Grandparents often suffer the most from the lack of thank-you's and recognition. They seem to be taken for granted more consistently than any other family member.

Grandma and the Sweaters

Once upon a time there was a wonderful Grandma. Before birthdays and holidays she knitted beautiful sweaters for her granddaughters, Anne, five, and Grace, three.

Knitting was something she liked to do so very much. She loved telling all her friends about her grandchildren as she knitted. When the girls' parents got divorced, the two children stopped sending Grandma thank-you notes.

After the second holiday and the second set of sweaters she knitted without response from the children, Grandma thought, "Well, I guess they've gotten too old for the sweaters, or they don't like them. Maybe they aren't the style." So she stopped knitting for them.

The grandchildren wished Grandma would knit new sweaters, but never mentioned it in the few phone conversations they had with her. She lived far away in Florida, and when she visited twice a year she brought them store-bought gifts.

The kids missed the sweaters and Grandma missed knitting them. They were all very sad. The sweaters were never mentioned again by Grandma or the girls.

5. Negotiating Family 2000

Family 2000 is the new millennium's family. Right now the traditional family—biological mother, father, and child—makes up only one-third of American families. In addition, research indicates that one-half of those now living in biologically connected families will divorce.

Remembering the definition of Family 2000—the divorced family, single mothers and dads who visit their children, and the recoupled, remarried, and/or stepfamily. Family 2000 makes up over 64 percent of our families today.

Family 2000 is extremely vulnerable to disintegration. According to Stepfamily Foundation statistics, 66 percent of remarriages end in breakup when children are actively involved.

Family 2000 cannot and will not function like the traditional family of the past. It has its own dynamics, its own line of development. It also has its own distinctive problems, one of which is that most people enter into it without knowing what to expect and how to find their way through its unfamiliar territory. The rules in this chapter are designed to provide a map and a guide.

Rule 35. Recognize That Biological and Sexual Bonds Are in Conflict in Family 2000.

"Love me, love my kids"? (Wrong!)

THE CONFLICT BEGINS WITH OUR GENES

One of the most important—and least understood—issues facing Family 2000 is the inherent conflict within the family system. The dynamic has its origins in our genes. In the original family, the couple comes together to have a child. The child is part of both parents. Mother and father are blood-bonded to the child. The child is part of them, and thus they work toward the well-being of the child. In step relationships, blood and sexual ties pull against each other. Our biological bonds—those with our child—are often in direct conflict with our sexual bonds—those with our new partner, new husband, or new wife.

To use a medical analogy, this is not unlike an organ transplant. In a transplant there occurs what doctors call "the rejection of nonself tissue." Doctors prepare for this biological phenomenon. They don't always succeed, but they are aware of the problem and address it. A similar dynamic of "rejection of the nonself" is neither understood nor anticipated by most who divorce and recouple. Indeed, it isn't even taught to the helping professionals who try to assist.

This concept can be difficult to understand. After all, our new partner loves us and knows that we come to him or her as a package deal—complete with one or more children. Yet when we marry or live together, many biological parents find ourselves confronting negative and rejecting feelings from our new partners toward the offspring of our previous marriage. In fact, stepparents rarely begin a new partnership without concerns about the children of a former partner. The child simply is not "part of" the stepparent.

It's not so different from what occurs in the animal kingdom, where many species reject the young that are not of their blood. In a lion pride a new male will actually kill the young cubs sired by a previous male, for instance. The females of very few species will nurse the young of another female. We are not animals, but our genetic programming is similar.

BLOOD TIES VERSUS SEXUAL TIES

The stepparent often feels that the child "gets in the way" of the new marriage. The biological parent is oversensitive and defensive. There are usually disagreements about discipline and procedures. Here's how a typical dialogue sounds:

"Your kids give us no privacy."
"Every time she comes over you pay no attention to me."
"I see my kid so little, why do you bug me about him?"
"If I don't give the kids what they want, they won't come to see me."

And on it goes—with the couple's conflicting reactions to the child or children often damaging their union.

Here is what one biological mother reported to me. Her ten-year-old son, Timmy, was late riding his bike home from school. She told her new husband of her fears about the road and the fact that it was getting dark. What if Timmy had been hit by a car! The stepfather replied, "We should be so lucky." She smacked him and they proceeded to have a two-day fight over his unkind words, his lack of caring, and his secret wish that the child didn't exist. Few stepparents speak as boldly as this man did, but many new stepparents feel that their relationships are being intruded upon by the child or children of a former marriage.

Divorce and remarriage are now social norms, yet our research shows that divorce is one of the deepest causes of lifetime suffering for both parents and children. Divorce is not a single painful event, but often an ongoing series of painful events. One of these is the formation of a stepfamily system, and in that system almost everyone experiences rejection.

Our research highlights the postdivorce problems for parent and child:

- Some 60 percent of children feel rejected by one of their parents, usually their father.
- An alarming number of children feel abandoned physically and emotionally by both parents.
- Some 50 percent of children see their mother or father undergo a second divorce.
- Their original parents provide less time, less discipline, and less sensitivity to the children because they are caught up in the divorce and its aftermath.
- As diminished parenting continues, it permanently disrupts the child-rearing functions of the family.

As a result of divorce, single moms most often have to work and/or seek another partner, while divorced dads often lessen their parenting efforts and become Disneyland dads and/or pal dads. What I am seeing—and this is a natural result of divorce— is more self-centeredness in parents, leading to more self-centeredness in children. Narcissism runs amok in our culture.

In more than twenty years of counseling, I have repeatedly seen how divorce shakes up parents' psyche and even relationship to their children. In an intact family, the focus is directed to the family as a unit. But, like a sledgehammer, divorce shatters the family and its focus. Forced now to function on his or her own, the divorced parent shifts his or her attention away from family and toward the self.

Strong, unified parenting—the kind that comes from the biological mother and father functioning as a unit—may also be lost. Very often, divorced parents remain angry with each other for years. And frequently the child is no longer the object of their joint efforts. Indeed, divorced parents may compete for the child's affections. Often the result is two child-dominated households.

Rule 36. Take Your Place as Head of the Household.

We must lead, guide, and parent no matter what the family structure!

Parenting is the hardest job any of us will ever do. The parent who must parent alone has a difficult job. But for the sake of the children, we must rise to the challenge.

SINGLE MOTHERS

Mothers who are parenting alone know all too well how difficult it is to take on the roles of both mother and father. The single mother must nurture and teach social skills—her traditional job—as well as teach the tough rules for competing, the father's traditional job. They must prepare the children for a world that now requires more work skills and more personal discipline. Very often they must take on the daunting task of single motherhood with considerably fewer financial resources than they had in their marriages.

Here are some important things to keep in mind:

- *Encourage your children's relationships with other author-ity figures.* Our research indicates that children of divorce participate in Scouts or after school teams at a lower rate than other children. That's not coincidental. When the kids complain about tough authority figures, too many parents let them quit. Instead, we should give them tips for getting along, disarming the coach with respect. Lord knows we have to learn to work with a lot of "mean" people in life.
- *Enroll Friends and relatives to help.* When I was a single mother, I often enlisted the help of male friends, uncles, and grandparents to fill the gap.

Male Authority and Lars

Uncle Jerry was a perfect example. So was my friend the legendary skier Stein Ericksen. One day when we were all skiing, my son Lars, then ten years old, fell. He lay on his back whimpering, too embarrassed to get up.

In the past when this happened, there would always be a big scene. I would pull, plead, and order him to stand up to no avail, Lars would just lie there sorrowfully and stubbornly. This time, instead of going back up the mountain myself I asked Stein: "Do something, please. Say something in male to him and get him up." (Yes, I do think "male" is a separate language.)

Stein climbed up the hill. From where we were standing, all we could see was Stein leaning over Lars. In short order Lars was up and the two of them were skiing down. They went right past me and got on the lift together.

Later, I asked Stein what he had said to Lars. He looked at me and smiled and then, in his marked Norwegian accent, repeated, "Vee men, when vee fall, vee get up!" Lars never did that again.

The point is powerful. Male authority carries weight and there is no getting around it.

I know many members of the feminist movement must be screaming, but I do believe that a lack of male authority figures is a major crisis in many young men's lives.

- *Don't share your adult concerns with your kids.* "Adult concerns" include your hurts, bad feelings, love stories, or relationship issues. Find a friend with whom to share these problems. When we make our concerns more important than our children and let them know it, they feel devalued. And since they can do nothing about our problems, they feel bad about themselves, and more alone.
- *Don't make your son the little man of the house.* He is still a child and needs to focus on his own activities. Too often, single mothers rely heavily on their boys to do the things around the house that their dad once did. Sure, having a son do some chores is appropriate, but he shouldn't be made to feel he has to take care of his mom. Her job is to take care of *him* and make him a good citizen of the household.
- *Money is never enough, so use it wisely.* Our research shows that 25 percent of the children of divorce suffer a severe and enduring drop in their standard of living. In addition, children of divorce tend to see a lasting difference between their mother's and father's standard of living.

    This is a time to help kids learn about earning money— baby-sitting, odd jobs for family friends, extra jobs around the house for extra money. Even though money often feels insufficient, do your very best *not* to create a feeling of scarcity in your home. Remember all those Depression babies? No matter how much they finally got, it was never enough. In contrast, we all know families in which there was a feeling of plenty, even when there was little money. That's because the parent conveyed to the children the feeling that "We have enough. We're fine. We'll make it. We love each other." When we love each other and care for each other there is abundance. Real scarcity is the lack of love and respect—no matter how much money there is.

FATHERS WHO VISIT THEIR CHILDREN

The majority of kids today are parented by one biological parent and visit the other parent perhaps every other weekend. The noncustodial parent, usually the dad, often feels he has too little time with the kids. He feels guilty. He does not want to spend his precious time with his children disciplining, and as a result he is an ineffective father.

In the worst cases, children of divorce don't even see the divorced dad. Studies show that these children, without the presence of a father or father figure, "do poorly" in life. This is especially true for boys.

- In our studies, 40 percent of young men aged nineteen to twenty-three from divorced families have no goals, a limited education, and a sense of having no control over their lives.
- Research shows that girls consistently adjust better and faster than boys do, both socially and academically— implying that boys may be suffering *more* than girls from the absence of their fathers.

Here are some important tips for fathers:

- *Take the reins.* Don't let kids stay up till all hours or let them watch adult movies. Sitting with them in front of a sports event on TV is not fathering.

- *Get out and do things together. You* are the coach. *Do. Don't just watch.* Teach them something—sports, fix-it skills, good manners, good sportsmanship.

- *Teach your children to respect authority.* Teach them respect for *your* authority. Too many fathers are put down and/or ordered around by their kids and don't even know it. Certainly they aren't objecting. That's not fathering. Of course kids can respectfully disagree, but they must not *command.*

- *Create a real bond with your kids.* Children need a meaningful connection with their father in order to grow up whole. The dad who just provides dinner, some small talk, or a sporting event for his visiting children is not fathering. Serving as an entertainment center is not the same as providing a home, building an intimate connection, teaching them something useful.

The Passport Story

When I was sixteen, I lived in Berlin with my mother. Whenever my father was there for business, we would meet. One day Dad said "How would you like to come to Monte Carlo on Friday? We'll stay at the Grand Hotel, see friends, go to the palace, and then go gambling in the famous Casino."

Gambling in Monte Carlo in the 1950s was not like today. It was right out of the pages of a fairy tale. Men wore dinner jackets and women wore long dresses. This was where the exciting people in Europe went to meet and play. I was just beginning to be impressed by the idea of dressing up and going to famous places. "Oh, of course I would," I said, "But I'm still on Mother's passport. Daddy, today is Tuesday—I can't get a new passport by Friday."

Of course I was thrilled, but how was I to get my very

own passport so fast? Then I had an idea. "Daddy, *you* know the consulate people. *You* could get me the passport!"

"Yes, but no," he said. I knew what he was about to do—give me another of his lessons in life. "This is for you to do." *"Why?"* I wailed. He just smiled. "Call me when you have the passport," he said and kissed me goodbye.

Did I hustle! I called the consulate. They told me it would take a few weeks. So I *went* to the consulate and pleaded in person with the secretary. As I was filling out the forms, I told her all about my dad and his exciting offer. I asked if she would please understand and could she possibly rush the process? I used my best child-of-divorce manipulation skills. In those days people weren't so busy and a polite and urgent young girl might just have a chance . . . She smiled at my efforts and said she would do her best.

On Thursday she called and asked me to come to the consulate. And there was my new passport with my picture. The number was handwritten.

I will never forget how proud I was of myself. My dad could easily have gotten the passport, or have had his secretary do it. But, typically he did not. He was always teaching me to be strong and independent.

Rule 37. The Rules for Visitation Must Be Clear, Predictable, and Consistent.

If a child lives with approval, he learns to like himself. If a child lives with overindulgence, he learns to dislike himself.

APPRECIATE THE STRESS FOR THE CHILD INVOLVED

Children travel between homes on a schedule few adults would endure. They shuttle back and forth between two part-time parents. We may sympathize with the corporate executive who must travel, but we expect children to adapt readily to moving from one house to another. Children must enter Mommy or Daddy's home and see Mommy or Daddy's new partner, and often *that* partner's children, and perhaps even a new baby, a half-brother or half-sister. Ughhhhhh . . . Put yourself in that child's place. What does he need? Predictability and love. Not overindulgence, but *love,* as shown in the care with which you handle this most sensitive of issues involving him: visitation.

- *Remember, you cannot control your child's behavior in the other parent's house.* There may be different rules at dad's house than there are at mom's house. And that's just the way it is. When kids are visiting your ex, there's little you can do about anything, no matter how inappropriate you think things are—from bedtime to eating habits. That is *their* house, *their* space. You can only manage *your* house and *your* space.
- *Visitation must be planned and agreements must be kept.* These are the golden rules of proper visitation. When these rules are broken, the child loses, self-esteem is damaged, and all parental relationships, both natural and step, are jeopardized.
- *The key to success is once again predictability and consistency.* Ideally, that means that the two of you confer about clothes needed, homework to be done, and what time Johnny will be picked up and brought back. If you are late or even "iffy" about your pickup time, you may well create a worried child. None of us likes to wait. By being late you are disrespecting your ex, and also your child.

CREATE ARRIVAL RITUALS

We plan for upcoming holidays and birthdays as a matter of course. In the same way, children should know when visitation will occur and should be encouraged to plan for it. The child needs to know what to expect. Surprises can be negative. Certain events should occur every time the child arrives for visitation. He should hang his coat in the same place and take his possessions to his room, for instance.

Closeness can be fostered at visitation with some sort of arrival ritual which includes, if possible, all members of the household— even if it's only the family sitting down to milk and cookies in the kitchen. This will become a happily anticipated beginning to a visitation. It is also a time to go over visitation plans. Arrival rituals diminish the awkwardness of not having been with each other for awhile and create a welcoming atmosphere for visitation.

The visiting child should have certain duties to perform— not so much because you need the help, but because these are his or her way of joining—becoming an active member of—the household.

Create a pattern that both you and the visiting child can follow, and punctuate that pattern with special times of closeness. Have ritual meals. Have time alone together—child and biological parent. Planning and allowing the child to know what will happen and what is expected of him are enormously important to a pleasant visitation experience.

KNOW THE RULES FOR THE VISITING PARENT

Do's

1. Do be on time when you pick up your child and return him on time.
2. Do be civil with your prior spouse. Too many exes don't talk at all. They're still too angry with each other. But no matter how bad the feelings or unpleasant the past, you should be cordial in front of the child and on the phone when the child is within earshot.
3. Do remember that when parents fight, the child feels bad about himself or herself.
4. Do integrate your child into your home.
5. Do spend time alone with your child—a lunch out together or a fifteen-minute walk off by yourselves, for instance.

Don'ts

1. Don't pump your child for information about the other parent.
2. Don't use your child as a messenger. (Remember, in ancient times the messenger who brought bad tidings was killed for his pains.)
3. Don't flaunt your new partner to your ex by taking him or her along when you pick up your child. If, however, there is an amiable relationship among all the adults, then going together should create no friction.
4. Don't make your child feel like a visitor.
5. Don't assume that your partner will take care of your child. You must be there if your child is visiting you.

Know the Rules for the Custodial Parent

The custodial parent also has a specific etiquette to follow which makes it easier for the child in visitation:

Do's

1. Do have your child ready on time for visitation.
2. Do make the experience of leaving for visitation as pleasant as possible.
3. Do be cordial with your prior spouse for the sake of the child's feelings.
4. Do let the child know that you will be okay while he is gone.
5. Do call your prior spouse as early as possible if visitation must be canceled or delayed.

Don'ts

1. Don't send your child out looking unkempt or without the right clothes for the weekend. Your intention may be to show how financially strapped you are, but you're punishing the child instead.
2. Don't send a sick child for visitation merely for the sake of convenience.
3. Don't tell your child that he doesn't have to listen to his or her stepparent.
4. Don't pump your child for information as to how the other half lives.
5. Don't bad-mouth your ex or anybody in the other home.

Rule 38. Learn to Co-Parent. It's Good for Your Kids.

Children of divorce do well when parents continue to parent, cooperate, and be faithful to "the best interests of the child."

BAD CO-PARENTING

It's an accepted fact of life that divorced parents usually fail to cooperate in co-parenting their children. Worse, many of them habitually argue, belittle each other, and refuse to talk to each other. But such "acting out" is for socially immature teenagers. Bad-mouthing and uncooperative divorced parents must *grow up* and recognize that, as mothers and fathers, we simply don't have the right to give voice to these feelings.

Our research shows that children of divorce tend to do well if mothers and fathers, regardless of remarriage, resume separate parenting roles, put differences aside, and allow the children to enjoy continuing relationships with the other parent. Unfortunately, only a few children have these advantages.

GOOD CO-PARENTING

Good co-parenting means working together for the best interests of the child. Conversation between exes should focus only on the child—not on money or personal resentments. Discussions between exes should be limited to questions regarding the child's school, health, extracurricular activities, and plans. There should be no recriminations and no negativity.

Rule 39. Don't Bad-Mouth Your Former Spouse.

I grew up to have my father's looks, my father's speech patterns, my father's opinions, and my mother's contempt for my father.

—Jules Fieffer

"Fifty percent of divorced women and 30 percent of divorced men were still intensely angry with their former spouses," according to research conducted by Judith Wallerstein. But when you behave badly toward your ex in front of the child or bad-mouth your ex to the child, you diminish yourself, your ex-partner, and most of all, the child. Good parents who value the best interests of the child find a way to manage their anger and be civil.

The children have already been traumatized by the divorce. They already know that their parents are not perfect. Why force them into the position of having to defend their other parent or, worse, feel bad and say nothing? A parent avoids criticizing the other parent, no matter how awful that person is, or was. Indeed, it's vital to find something good to say about that parent, because the child is made up of both of you. When we say something bad about the other parent, we are also hurting that child.

Rule 40. Explain the Divorce. Give Kids the Reasons.

They always say that time changes things, but you actually have to change them yourself.

—Andy Warhol

Go over the events surrounding the divorce with your children at least every two years. As children grow, their ability to understand evolves. Too often, we see parents telling their children, "It just didn't work out . . . We couldn't get along . . . We both love you . . . It's not your fault." This is not enough. Kids need to hear reasons. Otherwise, any time adults have a fight, children may fear that the adults will divorce. Reasons for the divorce need to have some substance—without bad-mouthing—so that kids can have some understanding of what took place. Without explanations, kids will experience anxiety every time an upset between people erupts.

Focus on Positive Differences

Explanations should tell a story focusing on positive character differences, rather than character flaws (even if the ex was the worst ever). For example a mother might say, "Daddy and I divorced because we could not agree on what to do. He wanted to work late and on weekends and I wanted to have him home and go out," while her ex-husband might say, "Mommy loved to have fun, talk on the phone, and be with her friends, while I wanted to stay home. I worked hard and I just wanted to rest." In providing such explanations, always do your best to secure the emotional stability of the child, *not* to put down your ex.

Rule 41. When Dating as a Single Parent, Be a Parent First.

If you think dating is tough, look at it from your kids' point of view!

How Dating Reactivates Feelings of Loss

Children of parents who are single, whether through divorce or death, are often fearful when the remaining parent goes out.

This is especially true for little ones who have no concept of time and who don't understand when or if you are going to come back. Older children also experience these anxieties. Your leaving the house may reactivate the earlier feelings of loss and abandonment.

Ways of Creating a Feeling of Safety for Your Kids

You may find your kids protesting your leaving. If you are picking up on their fear, you may in response find yourself leaving hurriedly to avoid a scene or staying home more often than is necessary. Instead, try sitting down to a "dinner before dinner"—a dirty-your-plate meal—with your kids before you go out (see page 000). Equally important, try to arrange things so that your child can follow the same predictable bedtime rituals on the nights you go out as on the nights you stay home. Too many of us cause our young ones undo upset by not getting them to bed early enough and going out in a hurried way that makes kids anxious.

Here are some other steps the single parent (usually mom) can take to create a feeling of safety for her child or children on the evenings she goes out.

1. If you are the type to make a fuss about getting dressed up to go out—which is natural and fun when there are no kids in the house—censor it. Your kids experience your excitement as a form of abandonment and rejection. Remember, they have not been invited. Make no fuss about yourself or the upcoming event.
2. It's good for kids to see a parent going out with friends.

Treat a "special date" as if it were of no more importance than going out with a pal.

3. If you are going out with a boyfriend, just tell the truth, "I am going to dinner with my friend Jerry and then we will go to a movie." *(No* "for grown-ups only" details about how cute he is and how much you like him.)

4. Present the date as a friend until the relationship becomes serious and long-term.

5. Don't show affection for your boyfriend in front of your children. And there should not be the slightest suggestion of sexual activity between the two of you. Not even vibes, unless the relationship is for real. Children pick up on adult sexual energy, and can make life very difficult for a lover out of fear of losing you.

6. Tell them what time you will be home—even if they will be sleeping when you return. This knowledge makes children feel safer. *Be* home at the time you say you will.

7. Unless this is a committed relationship, don't stay out overnight. This scares even the biggest of kids. If you're out all night, get up at dawn and go home to your own bed. In the same way, don't let kids find a lover in your bed. Children don't understand—even grown ones are often upset—and interpret your intense and sexual feeling for another as personal loss. They feel that someone else is more important than they are in your life.

8. Don't let your children in on your loneliness or your sexual conquests. Again, such information is threatening to children. They feel displaced, even feel betrayed. This in turn may express itself as contempt for your date—even when it's someone they've never met. And what if this date eventually becomes a stepparent? The hostility will already be built in, and such feelings are difficult to change.

"Hi. What's Your Name?"

In the early days of my parents' divorce—when I was about twelve—my father frequently had a woman stay overnight while I was visiting him. My being there did not stop him. So, in the morning I would prance into his bedroom, look down at the lady beside him and say, "Hi. What's *your* name?" She would tell me. Then I would return with, "Oh, Mary was here last week." That usually got her to leave in a hurry, And I'd have Dad all to myself. (I never said I wasn't a wicked stepchild.) Dad soon learned that when I visited it was not safe for him to have overnight guests.

Too often, single parents do have sleep over guests, and too often, kids say nothing. Limit your overt sexuality when kids are around. Many kids feel the charge, feel left out, feel sad—or like me, try to get rid of the interloper.

Rule 42. Be Clear About Who Comes First and When: Your Partner or Your Kids?

Seldom or never does a marriage develop into an individual relationship smoothly and without crisis.
—C.G. Jung

When you're dating, your kids come first. When you're recoupled and in a committed relationship, the partnership comes first. Kids must be taught to express respect—whether or not they feel it—for the new male or female head of household and accept the fact that he or she comes first.

Dividing Your Time Among Family Members

Organize time alone with your partner, organize time alone with your kids, and organize time together as a family. Even in a traditional family, parents have to schedule time to be alone together, and mothers and fathers each need time to bond with their children individually. It's the same in the stepfamily only more so. Remember, the stepfamily isn't like the traditional family, where the whole group is happy to be together. The biological parent must divide his time among family members. Here's an example: Dad's sixteen-year-old daughter comes for a weekend. He can take her out to lunch by himself on Saturday; the couple can go out alone together Saturday night; and everyone can be together for brunch on Sunday.

The Changing Dynamics of a New Family

Who do you answer first when both your mate and your child call? This situation can be ripe for conflict. Somebody has to come first. You can scream for mercy, or you can take the approach that you only have two ears and one mind, that adults come first, and that nobody interrupts. Traditionally, families have ranked the importance of their various members on the basis of age. Although your child may have come first while you two were on your own, the dynamics of the situation change once the step- or recoupling relationship is established. Children now have to defer to the new male or female household head.

Rule 43. Be Aware That Recoupling Can Be Hazardous to Your Sex Life.

The newer the relationship, the harder you have to work at playing.

THE TUG-OF-WAR BETWEEN PARENTING AND ROMANCE

Acquiring an instant family, complete with children, can seriously hamper sexuality. In any relationship, adjusting to each other is an enormous challenge. But with the additional adjustment of children, what chance does your sex life have? This is especially true for the divorced mom or dad with children sleeping in the next room.

The key to dealing with the tug-of-war between parenting and romance is to set priorities, to organize, and to face facts. Talk over with your partner the demands that a child makes, both on you and on the relationship. The step relationship is not based exclusively on romance. Parenting and stepparenting play a major role. That reality must be squarely faced and accepted.

MAKING TIME TO BE ALONE TOGETHER

The child has to give a little in this situation as well. Let your children know that they are loved very much and that no one is going to take that away. Let them know equally clearly, however, that they are no longer the only people with claims on your time, that the family now includes a new member who isn't going to go away, and that, as much as you love them, you also love your new partner and you want your children to respect that.

Couples who are remarried need to spend time alone and out of the house. Often they feel too guilty to go out when kids are visiting. However, if your kids visit regularly and for long Friday-through-Sunday weekends, it's good for you to have a date night after the relationships are established.

Rule 44. Establish the Adults' Bedroom-Door Rule.

There are only two occasions when Americans respect privacy—prayer and fishing!

—Herbert Hoover

THE IMPORTANCE OF PRIVACY

In a step relationship—as opposed to the original family—the partnership is exciting and new, and therefore there is a need for greater privacy. But there is also the presence of prying youngsters who would often like nothing better than to have Mom or Dad alone, minus the new partner. This is yet another reason for privacy and boundaries. The bedroom-door rule was not that important in your biological family. Even as single parents, you allow, or allowed, kids access to your bedrooms. The sanctity of this private adult space becomes vital, however, when you have a new partnership to nurture.

The Bedroom-Door Rule

Here is how the bedroom-door rule worked in our family:

1. When the bedroom door is open, a child may announce him or herself, and say, "May I come in?" as he or she enters.
2. When the door is ajar, the child must knock and enter only after being given permission by an adult.
3. When the door is closed, the child may not come in unless the house is burning down.

The Lesson of Boundaries

You, as the couple, must establish privacy. Why? As the poet Robert Frost said, "Good fences make good neighbors." So, too, do good boundaries between parents and children make for good households. It's simply not good for children—or parents—to allow kids to enter the parental bedroom at will. This isn't to say that you shouldn't have your kids bouncing on the bed and cuddling with you. But it's up to *you*—not your kids—to decide when and how you'll play with them.

Remember, a child's priority is gaining power over his parents. That's the way God made us. The fact is, achieving power over their parents is what all animals at some time or another try to do. Loving a child is teaching him that he is not the one who rules the house. If, on the contrary, we teach kids that they can run things, why should they ever learn something uncomfortable or hard from an adult? Or for that matter learn anything in life that is uncomfortable?

We see them out there, the "no" people. They struggle with employers, coaches, and teachers. They don't listen. They're often unable to be good workers. Bosses find them unmanageable. In short these "no" people are not surviving. They were not trained to. Their parents failed.

The bedroom door issue is a powerful metaphor for rules, boundaries, and who decides them. It's also good preparation for life.

Rule 45. Understand the Kids' Conflict of Loyalties.

If at first you don't succeed, you're running about average

This conflict, particular to step relationships, causes a round-robin of confused emotions. Often, just as the child in a stepfamily begins to have warm feelings toward the stepparent, he will pull away and act out negatively. He often feels: "If I love you, that means I don't love my real parent." The question of "Who am I loyal to first?" goes all the way around in the stepfamily.

The feelings are normal and must be dealt with. Gently explain to your child that it's possible to establish new loving relationships. For example, you might say, "The heart has many sections for loving, and the sections grow as you grow. You have one mommy and one daddy, and nobody will ever take their place. It's okay, though, to care about your stepparent too."

Rule 46. Recognize That "Becoming One Big Happy Family" Is Highly Unlikely

The greatest discovery of my generation is that a human being can alter his life by altering his attitudes of mind.
—William James

One big happy family? Believe me, it ain't gonna happen. And when it doesn't, you shouldn't blame each other and each other's children.

"THE BRADY BUNCH" MYTH

Perhaps we'd all secretly like to be like the stepfamily in the TV series, *The Brady Bunch*. In twenty-four minutes, Mr. and Mrs. Brady used to solve all their children's problems. Neither the couple nor their kids seemed to be affected by any of the usual dynamics of stepfamilies. Indeed, whatever tiffs there were were quickly resolved, and everything went back to being warm and pleasant. Unfortunately, many of the children I counsel watch reruns of *The Brady Bunch* enviously, and feel terrible that their family doesn't interact like the Bradys.

But it's unrealistic to expect a "Brady Bunch" situation. We can't blend the Smiths and the Joneses into one big happy family. For the sake of our kids, it should be pointed out just how simpleminded the thinking behind *The Brady Bunch* really is.

DEVELOPING COUPLE STRENGTH

There are those who say it just takes time for the stepfamily to develop and cohere. We say it takes education and sometimes counseling. The stepfamily doesn't have years to grow with each other, the way a biological family does. Instead, a working team must be created, and quickly. The couple has to decide—up front—how duties, responsibilities, manners, discipline, money, inheritances, and other aspects of life are to be handled.

In step relationships, only a very few "big, happy" families evolve naturally. It's up to you and your spouse to take the lead in setting the family guidelines and declaring firmly what you will and will not allow in your household. Creating the rules and enforcing them means that you also have to develop *couple strength*. Couple strength is important to your marriage, of course, but it's also vital to the stability of your stepfamily. You will find that many of your decisions will be unpopular, even bitterly resented. But as long as you and your spouse are united in mutual love and respect, *your family will weather the storm.*

Rule 47. Have Realistic Expectations.

Unrealistic expectations beget rejections and resentments.

OVERCOMING PROBLEMS BY IDENTIFYING THEM

The desire to make the stepfamily mimic the biological family creates a whole range of false expectations such as we will be one big, happy family, we will get a new mom or dad, and we will be just like the Brady Bunch—solving all of our problems without family conflict and within a half-hour. These false expectations also lead to a denial of the many adjustments that stepfamily members must make. The way to overcome problems is to identify them. Most of the problems in stepfamilies stem from a failure to acknowledge that the step situation does, indeed, create a special need for education and understanding.

THE NEED FOR NEW MODELS

For most children the recoupling cements the loss of their original family and often begins with a dislike of the new stepparent. Not only does the new family consist of different and unrelated members, it also must be explained and managed differently.

Generally, there is no model for the step relationship other than in fairy tales, where the stepparent is wicked and cruel and the real parent is ineffectual or absent. The Stepfamily Foundation has created new models. Reading this book is educating yourself.

Rule 48. Blame the Step Situation, Not the People Involved.

What counts . . . is not so much how compatible you are, but how you deal with incompatibility.
—George Levinger

A big mistake stepfamilies make is blaming themselves and each other for the feelings and difficulties that are intrinsic to the step situation. Blame not only makes you feel helpless, but, like guilt and recrimination, only delays finding solutions.

Stepchildren are often blamed for family problems, but this only disguises the true source of the problems. It's never easy being the child in a step relationship. Complicating this, the child may, consciously or unconsciously, derive a sense of power as a child of death or divorce. Naturally, he wants to defend his territory. This behavior can result in real pain for both the biological parent and the stepparent.

While no one will deny that the presence of stepchildren makes the relationship a more difficult and complex one, blaming the children only denies your power to change things. Only you have the responsibility for the success or failure of your stepfamily. Only you can establish the guidelines—and guide the children in becoming part of that relationship.

Rule 49. Remember That There Are No Ex-Parents, Only Ex-Spouses.

My mom says my dad is no good.
My dad says my mom is no good.
I say I'm no good.
And I'm probably right . . .

PARENTS ARE FOREVER

How should you deal with your prior spouse? The answer is "very carefully." Like it or not, parents are forever. Although your ex may continually intrude on your efforts to create a new life and may try to run your home and children as well, you must try to place these dynamics in context. The prior spouse *is* your child's biological parent, and the blood ties are emotionally charged. There is no getting around it.

Admittedly, you might resent your former husband or wife for meddling in your affairs and trying to influence your children in various ways, including bad-mouthing you, your new partner, or your friends. But remember, everyone in the family of divorce has suffered a loss. The hurt exists on all fronts. Even when your ex is inconsiderate or angry, the worst thing you can do is react in kind in front of your children. It damages them.

The Stepparent—Always One Step Removed

If you are a new partner, you must recognize the hard fact that the children are not yours and never will be. You are a stepparent, not a replacement parent. *Mother* and *Father* (no matter how awful they may be) are sacred concepts and arouse intense feelings. Respect the child's need to love that parent. It is instinctual and natural. As a stepparent, you are a step removed, yet in this position you can still play a significant role in the development of the child. As a stepparent, you can become a loved, respected mentor to the child, but not if you show disrespect for the place the biological parent holds in the child's heart.

Rule 50. Learn How to Exorcise Ghosts . . . Delicately

The strongest of all warriors are these: time and patience.

When a parent has died, children's memories are complicated, and myths may arise. In some cases, the widow or widower also idealizes the former spouse, making the going very rough for a new partner.

Respect the Child's Memories

Children, especially stepchildren, tend to gild every memory of their late parent. One stepchild talked frequently of her late mother, someone she remembered as a beautiful woman who was loved by everyone she met. She was gracious, adored, and kind, and the child said that she missed her terribly. You would never guess that she was all of six months old when her mother died. As the stepparent to this child, or anyone like her, there is nothing you can say that will combat the myth. It would be cruel even to try. Let the child sustain the myth. This is necessary to the child's self-esteem. Respect his or her feelings. Reassure the child that you understand, and that you aren't going to try to replace the lost parent; no one could. Show the child that you don't want to push the memory of the late parent away. For example, I suggest that the two of you go shopping for a beautiful frame for a favorite picture of the absent parent. Then help the child find a place in his or her room for the framed picture.

MAKE CHANGES SLOWLY

Ideally, every new family—but especially one in which the prior spouse has died, should have a new home. Economically, it's not always feasible. So, if you do move into the home that the prior spouse decorated, maintained and lived in, go slowly in attempting to make it your own.

Most children dislike change and are attached to the way their home looks. But beyond that, redecorating immediately may be seen as a great insult to the absent parent. It may even shake up your new spouse. Changes will have to be made, but delicacy is required. Get your spouse and especially the children in on the redecorating. When the children help, they can more easily accept the changes, and, by extension, you.

Rule 51. Know the Stepparent's Role in Discipline.

Don't become a stereotype stepparent. Break the mold!

The stepparent *cannot* play an independent role in discipline. Remember that the couple decides on the rules of the house (see Rule 17, page 41, and the Family Rules Chart, pages 162–164). The rules are presented at a family meeting, and then the stepparent may say, "Your dad and I have decided that . . ."

AVOID TELLING KIDS WHAT TO DO

Stepparents are often given the bad advice that they can set family rules and discipline on their own. Sadly, whether it is good parenting or not, the stepparent telling kids what to do is the fastest way to become the cruel stereptype. Watch it! Taking charge may lead to nothing but "You are *not* my parent and you *can't* tell me what to do," from the stepchildren.

Let's say that fifteen-year-old Tim has taken his morning shower. Dad has already left for work. Stepmom is getting ready to leave. Tim has left his wet towels on the bathroom floor. (This is often a test by the kid. I know—I tried them all.) Stepmom walks by, remembers the rules they went over, and knowing her role, says kindly but firmly, "Tim, you know that your dad and I have decided towels go on the towel rack, so I guess those towels on the floor go on your rack." This should get Tim to pick up his stuff. If not, she may have to push Tim a little bit, but without raising her voice. Raising her voice would mean that she had lost her temper—and thus her power—and Tim would have won the encounter. She might try this: "Tim, please don't make me tell Dad that you broke the rules. I hate to see you lose privileges. Towels on the rack, man."

WHEN YOU GET ANGRY, IT SHOWS WEAKNESS AND THE CHILD IS IN CONTROL

Even if a stepchild is doing something outrageous, you must do your best *not* to shoot from the hip and show anger. Remember, kids will test to see if they can get you angry and to check out who comes first with their biological parent—the child or the stepparent. Children jockey for power with a stepparent in a way they never would with a biological parent. *Don't* lose your temper.

For example, you can say something like, "Mary, I don't think your dad would approve of you having your boyfriend in your room with the door closed." Say it in as neutral a voice as possible. "Shall I call him so we can find out? Do you want to wait until he comes home and ask? Or would you two like to go downstairs in the family room until we find out?"

Rule 52. Give Special Thanks to Stepparents.

Don't let yourself or someone else be taken for granted.

Very little in a stepfamily can be taken for granted. When a biological mom or dad does something nice for the kids, it's just taken for granted as being part of their job. But stepparents need to be thanked for doing things that the biological parent does naturally and without acknowledgment. The parent can easily view his child as an extension of himself. As a result, tasks performed for biological children come more easily. This doesn't mean that stepparents are cruel or indifferent. Being selfless is simply more difficult with a stepchild than with one's own child. Stepparent and stepchild can and do learn to love each other. I loved my stepfather. It takes time and work.

Making Thanks a Part of Your New Family Language

Children may find thank-yous alien to their vocabulary unless they are taught otherwise. When the stepparent performs tasks that are naturally handled by the biological parent, the child is even less likely to say, "Thank you." It's important to make thanks a vital part of your new family "language." It's one of the simplest and most basic changes you and your partner will have to establish, and it will pave the way for other constructive attitudes within the step situation.

Rule 53. Remember That Grandparents Have a Special Role.

When grandparents lose out, so do kids.

In the hectic business that surrounds divorce and remarriage, the roles played by grandparents and other relatives in the child's extended family are often forgotten. This is very unfortunate, because the child continues to need the warmth and love that these other relatives can provide. In many cases, the child loses all contact with the grandparents or other family from the noncustodial side of the family. Even if this is not the case right after the divorce, it often becomes true when the custodial parent remarries.

Grandparents Represent a Special Kind of Love

As a rule, grandparents fare badly in the step situation. So do their grandchildren if the two are pulled apart. Grandparents are valuable to the child because they represent a special kind of love. They adore their grandchildren without asking first if they are getting good grades in school and without checking whether they have straightened up their rooms. The love and sharing of grandparents with their grandchildren is a combination of warmth, doting, care-taking, pride, and concern. When we take away a child's grandparents, we take away plenty.

Although the wishes of the biological parent have traditionally dictated the extent to which grandparents may visit grandchildren, this is changing. The courts are beginning to recognize the psychological value of continuity in a child's life, and grandparents are an important part of this. They may even be a primary source of comfort and security in the immediate aftermath of a divorce.

6. Tools for Family 2000

What follows are the tools and skill-building exercises we have learned and invented over the years in working with couples to assist them and their families. These skill-building techniques often relate to working out conflicts and what we call "honoring the differences."

Each tool relates to a rule. Use them when you want hands-on help in working out the complexities of your Family 2000. Follow the instructions and *have fun*.

Tools for Partnering

(Use with Rule 8. Learn the new partnering. It's the secret key to success.)

THE MULTIPLE-POINT-OF-VIEW APPROACH

A very important part of our work in guiding Family 2000 is getting across the idea of multiple points of view. We believe that before we can resolve differences, we must respect them. This is essential. We each have our own way of doing things and our own beliefs about discipline, meals, roles, and a hundred other things.

There's an old saying that goes, "Conflicts are caused by not honoring our differences." This holds true for all relationships, but is especially important to Family 2000. It is a vital concept for new partners and for divorced spouses who may be tempted to tell their children "bad things" about their former partner.

Let's say you discover that your ex has been criticizing you to your children. You should tell them that, while you defend their other parent's first-amendment right to say what he or she feels, they must also hear how *you* saw, heard or felt things, such as why you divorced (this without disparaging or bad-mouthing), or your values and expectations about day-to-day living. Try saying, "This is my reality. It's not your job to decide who's right or wrong. Your job as our children is to respect and listen to and to honor each parent's point of view. "You may never know the truth. Only God knows, and She isn't talking!"

One History, Different Points of View

I went to high school in three different countries. The history I was taught was very different in each country. At first I naively made note to my teachers that other countries had different versions of the same story. They ignored me. Then I wrote a paper describing these differences. I got a reprimand—"This was not the assignment!"—and a low grade. So I stopped this comparison business. I decided that history was a point of view and not just the facts, and that it varied country to country, teacher to teacher.

Actually, this rude awakening was not such a bad thing. My divorced parents were still angry at each other. Each constantly told me a different story about the other. My school experiences helped me to deal with the conflicts between my parents. I began to view my parents as conflicting societies experiencing history from different points of view. I was relieved of the awful curse of feeling that I had to take sides, to believe one parent over the other.

THE A/B REALITY TOOL

One of the most important tools we use here at the Stepfamily Foundation is our A/B Reality Tool. I draw two boxes—one marked with a big *A* and the other with a big *B*. I explain that each of us is programmed differently: A likes pink flowers, B likes red flowers. A does not like to sunbathe, B loves the sun. B argues, "A, you'd look great with a tan. Come with me to the beach, and let's enjoy the sun together." "No," says A. "You are a dope to lie in the sun." Each tries to pull the other into his or her reality. Each argues his or her point of view.

The challenge for both is to create a *C* reality in their partner-ship. To do this, they must take some from *A*'s reality and some from *B*'s reality. Agreements to disagree become agreements and go into the *C* column until every major conflict is worked out. *Note:* Both partners avoid using the word "you" while doing this exercise. Language like, "You don't know what you're talking about! *This* is the reality!" is not allowed. Remember, we are learning to understand a third language—not "Yours" or "Mine," but "Ours." As in a foreign country, showing courtesy in any communication exchange is imperative.

It *is* okay to use the word "I," as in "I feel . . . I see . . . I hear . . ." We own and honor the reality as our own. We recognize that the other is not wrong, but simply different.

How We Experience People, Places, and Things Differently

Following is an exercise that illuminates the differences in the ways individuals see, hear, and feel their world, and how differently they rate their experiences of the same people, places, and things. Some people, for instance, consider that it's been a good day if they've been with people they like. Some people consider it a good day if they've been in a beautiful place. Still others consider it a good day if they've been out driving their Mercedes—i.e., for them, the quality of the *things* they deal with defines the experience.

Lake Placid: One Trip, Two Realities

My husband is the usual guinea pig for these training exercises I learn at professional training seminars. Once, after skiing the whole day at Lake Placid, I asked him if he would endure an experiment during our journey from the door of the hotel to a restaurant where we were dining that night. "Yes," he laughed, with a little trepidation.

"We'll notice what we see, hear, and feel," I said. "We'll do this silently on the way and discuss it when we sit down at the restaurant." "Blessings," he cried, happy that this was to be such an uncomplicated exercise. We followed through with the plan and, once seated in the restaurant, he said, "You start." I did.

My Reality

We went out the hotel door. It was freezing cold. Ice was on the steps down to the car. He held my arm to help me into the car. "How nice," I thought, "I was falling all over the mountain during the day, and he never offered to pick me up. Well, we're both tough skiers." I was dressed for dinner. I remember nothing of the drive except that the night was black. We pulled into the parking lot, and I could hear the gravel under the car wheels. We walked up the steps to the restaurant. A blond, buxom lady led us to our table. I smelled the room, thinking the food would be only mediocre, and looked around at the people—pretty mediocre also.

His Reality

Interestingly enough, his memory didn't include helping me into the car or anything about the drive to the restaurant. But after getting to the restaurant and pulling into the parking lot, he did notice how many other BMWs were in the parking lot and that the license plates were from different states. How many from Canada? Massachusetts? New York? Vermont? New Jersey? He didn't notice the blond lady who took us to our table.

I was astounded. How different we are! I would never have noticed the things he noticed. Men spend so much time thinking about how they measure up to other men. (Who else had a BMW? How far did others have to drive to get there?) While I had *heard* the noises in the parking lot, he *saw* what was in it. He was thinking about *things*. I was thinking about *feelings* and *people*.

So, here are your *instructions:* Drive, walk, or otherwise go somewhere together without talking, and when you arrive, compare what you observed. Have fun!

Walk a Mile in the Other's Shoes—High Heels or Cordovans

The following exercise involves actually becoming your partner's shadow in movement and in spirit. The two of you go for a walk in an area where there are people, stores, or things with which to interact. When your partner stares at something, you stare at the same thing. No matter how long she looks at something or interacts with someone, stand by her and observe. Attempt to feel what is going on in her. What's important to her? Why does she like to do this? What's nice for her? What's difficult for you? What insights do you get about you and your partner?

This is really getting to know each other by observing. So, no laughing, unless she does, and no putdowns. The "follower's" job is to be silent and to "be with . . ." The "walker's" job is just to be herself and to do as she would normally do on her own. As the follower, give most of your attention to observing the other, but in one corner of your mind think about what *you'd* like and would want to do or say under the same circumstances.

Walk the way he walks. Look at what he looks at, feel what he touches. Stay right with him, saying nothing. Be his shadow. Your job is to learn, know, be like, be him. You see, hear, feel as he does.

Don't forget to have fun! This is your partner, and, using this exercise, you can find out astonishing similarities and dissimilarities in the way each of you views the world. We may not exactly understand our differences, but we can respect them.

Here are your instructions: Do this exercise for about twenty minutes at a time. It can be done anytime you both go for a walk, to the mall, to the seashore, or other places you visit together. Each partner takes a ten-minute turn. Compare your insights after each is finished. Enjoy.

Calling a Time-Out

Often, during a disagreement, one party wants to persist and pursue the issue longer than the other. The other may feel overwhelmed and start to fight or withdraw. Before either begins to yell or argue, it's helpful to call a time-out. This can be done with prearranged hand signals—perhaps the ones used by referees in football games—or with prearranged words that stop the action.

When a time-out is called, decide on another specific time when the discussion will be resumed. Make that date, and allow each other the time-out, knowing there will be another time to have your say.

MAKE IT A DATE

Following the first romantic stage of a relationship, couples can get bogged down in the mundane. The first bloom fades, and many couples feel they have lost some of the intense love they shared. But you fell in love once, and the qualities that led to the initial attraction are still there. With tenacity, time, and improved communication, that love can be rekindled.

Have an evening out together every week. The date must be a priority each week. Take at least three hours, and spend it on neutral ground. It cannot be at home. Try a public place like a restaurant or a movie and something to eat afterward. Don't talk about family issues. Talk about the movie, politics, ideas—anything but family problems.

PARTNERSHIP ISSUES TO BE RESOLVED

In every partnership, there are conflicts and issues to be resolved. We have found that it's extremely helpful to write them down. The act of writing helps you clarify problems and make your issues specific. You'll get the best results if you each make your own list. Each of you should also number your issues, starting with the one you think is easiest to solve, and progressing to the hardest. Note and discuss how differently each of you views the priorities and problems and which ones you each think are easiest and hardest to resolve.

Here are your instructions: Each of you writes a specific list of partnership issues (which can range from the discipline of children to the allocation of money and/or time together, from who walks the dog, pays the bills, and cleans the bathroom, to much more). Next, each of you numbers the items on his or her list, with number 1 being the easiest issue to resolve and number 10 being the hardest. Naturally, your lists won't match up, number for number! Perhaps you put "Jamie's soccer practice" first, and your partner lists "cooking dinner." Simply alternate, discussing *your* number 1, then your *partner's* number 1, then your number 2 and your partner's number 2, etc. *Note:* A decision *not* to decide an issue now is a decision.

His Issues to Be Resolved

1.

2.

3.

4.

5.

6.

7.

8.

9.

10.

Her Issues to Be Resolved

1.

2.

3.

4.

5.

6.

7.

8.

9.

10.

TIME-ENERGY-MONEY CHART

Partnering today is hard work and involves many roles. Often, one member of the couple feels that he or she does too much and the other not enough. Remember the information in the rule about partnering that we need a secretary, nanny, yard worker, maid, etc.?

The Time-Energy-Money Chart will help you figure out just exactly how each sees his or her responsibilities and jobs and how each sees the other's responsibilities and jobs. *Note:* When one person spends much time at work and makes a greater proportion of money, he or she may choose to hire out, or pay someone to do a job, if that is possible.

Here are your instructions: Begin by making a second copy of the Time-Energy-Money Chart, so that you'll each have one. Fill them out separately. When you've each completed your chart, compare. Notice the differences in your hours of time, percentages of energy, and amounts of money. Figure out some resolutions. Agree, agree to agree on your differences, or agree to disagree. Don't fight. Just honor the differences in perception.

Time-Energy-Money Chart

	TIME	ENERGY	MONEY
HOME			
BASIC CONTRIBUTION			
MAINTENANCE			
INSIDE WORK			
OUTSIDE WORK			
UPGRADING			
ENTERTAINING			
MEALS			
CAREER			
MINE			
PARTNER'S			
CHILDREN: MINE			
AS CARETAKER			
AS TEACHER			
IN PLAY			
PARTNER'S			
AS CARETAKER			
AS TEACHER			
IN PLAY			
OURS			

AS CARETAKER			
AS GUIDE			
IN PLAY			
PRIOR SPOUSE			
MINE			
PARTNER'S			
PLAYTIME			
WITH PARTNER			
ALONE			
WITH MY CHILDREN			
WITH PARTNER'S CHILDREN			
WITH OUR CHILDREN			
LEARNING AND GROWTH			
PERSONAL			
PERSONAL JOINT			

Tools for Money Management

(Use with Rule 9. Manage Your Money. Don't Just Expect That "It Will All Work Out.")

The following forms—the Asset and Debt Statement, the Expense Information Worksheet, and the Installment Payments List—are used as complete-disclosure documents between couples. So often we find that, without complete disclosure, there can be unrealistic expectations about the allocation of money by one partner or the other. Filling out these documents can help take the guesswork out of money allocation and enable Family 2000 couples to make considered decisions about their spending, based on a thorough review of their financial responsibilities for such things as child support, health care, education costs, and so forth.

Asset and Debt Statement

Here are your instructions: Begin by making a second copy of the form so that you'll each have one. Fill them out separately. Then compare and correlate your answers. *Note:* You'll need to gather your documents—divorce and child care agreements, stock statements, etc.—before completing the statement.

I. SEPARATE PROPERTY (Yours only): Possessions, money, and real estate that you owned prior to this marriage, received as gifts or inheritances, or obtained after you separated.

a) Real estate

Address: _____

Estimated fair market value: _____

Loan amounts: _____

Estimated equity: _____

Address: _____

Estimated fair market value: _____

Loan amounts: _____

Estimated equity: _____

Address: _____

Estimated fair market value: _____

Loan amounts: _____

Estimated equity: _____

b)   Money: Bank accounts and cash

Location   Account #   Current Balance

_____

_____

_____

_____

_____

_____

_____

c)   Stocks, bonds, and limited partnerships

Name   Current Value

_____

_____

_____

_____

_____

_____

_____

_____

_____

d)   Secured and unsecured notes

Borrower   Due Date   Current Balance

_____

_____

_____

_____

_____

e)   Tax refunds due

Year   Date Expected   Amount Due

_____

_____

_____

_____

f)   Retirement, pension, profit-sharing, and annuities

Name of Plan   Current Balance

_____

_____

_____

_____

_____

g)   Life insurance

Carrier   Beneficiary   Cash Value, if any   Face Value

_____

_____

_____

_____

_____

h)   Business interests

Name of Company   Date Acquired   Estimate of Value

_____

_____

_____

_____

_____

i)   Household furniture, furnishing, and appliances

_____

_____

_____

_____

_____

_____

j)   Cars, trucks, boats

Year____Make_____   Estimated Value   Loan Balance

Equity

_____

_____

_____

_____

_____

_____

_____

II.   PROPERTY IN THIS MARRIAGE: Possessions, money, and real estate that you own JOINTLY and that are not your separate property.

_____

_____

_____

_____

_____

_____

_____

_____

_____

III.   SEPARATE DEBTS: (Incurred by you before marriage, during last marriage, or during this marriage)

Creditor's Name   Balance Owing

_____

_____

_____

_____

IV.   PAST MARRIAGE OBLIGATIONS: (Incurred at divorce; alimony, obligations toward children, health care, camp, college etc.

Name   Amount Estimated

_____

_____

_____

_____

_____

_____

_____

_____

_____

_____

_____

EXPENSE INFORMATION WORKSHEET

Here are your instructions: Once again, begin by making a second copy of the form so that you'll each have one. Fill them out separately. Then compare and correlate your answers.

Name _____

MONTHLY EXPENSES	CURRENT	FUTURE
1. Residence payments		
a) Rent or mortgage	$_____	$_____
b) Property taxes and insurance	$_____	$_____
c) Maintenance	$_____	$_____
2. Food (at home and household supplies)	$_____	$_____
3. Food (eating out)	$_____	$_____
4. Gas, electricity, water, trash, cable TV	$_____	$_____
5. Telephone	$_____	$_____
6. Laundry and cleaning	$_____	$_____
7. Clothing	$_____	$_____

8. Medical, including insurance $_____ $_____

9. Dental, including insurance $_____ $_____

10. Life insurance $_____ $_____

11. Child care $_____ $_____

12. Children's extra-curricular activities $_____ $_____

13. Education:

     a) Self $_____ $_____

     b) Children $_____ $_____

14. Entertainment:

     a) Self $_____ $_____

     b) Children $_____ $_____

15. Transportation and auto expenses:

     a) Insurance $_____ $_____

     b) Gas $_____ $_____

     c) Repair and maintenance $_____ $_____

     d) Transportation (e.g., commuting costs) $_____ $_____

16. Installment payments $_____ $_____

    (insert total and itemize

    below)

17. Incidentals:

    a) Gifts $_____ $_____

    b) Subscriptions $_____ $_____

    c) Haircuts, etc. $_____ $_____

    d) Vacations $_____ $_____

    e) Travel to be with chil- $_____ $_____

    dren

    f) $_____ $_____

    g) $_____ $_____

TOTAL MONTHLY EXPENSES $_____ $_____

INSTALLMENT PAYMENTS LIST

Here are your instructions: Make a second copy of the form, so that you'll each have one. Fill them out separately. Then compare and correlate your answers. (Put a *C* by debts you consider couple debts, and an S by debts you consider your separate debts.)

CREDITOR'S NAME-C/S	PAYMENT FOR	MONTHLY PAYMENT	BALANCE OWING
1.			
2.			
3.			
4.			
5.			
6.			
7.			
8.			
9.			
10.			

Tools for Constructing Your Vision of the Family

(Use with Rule 16. Have a Vision of How You Would Like Your Family to Work and Behave Together.)

In a step relationship, whether you're married or living together, you really need to find out who you are as a couple and define your expectations for the relationship. Human families are complex, and they become even more so when they involve recoupling and stepchildren. This can prove very confusing when so many of our expectations are based on the traditional family model.

Before combining with another person to create a new family, it's a good idea to think about your own and your partner's expectations. How are your two visions of the stepfamily different? How are they the same? The following exercise can help you understand the similarities and differences in your individual views.

YOUR VISION OF THE FAMILY

Here are your instructions: Again, make a second copy of the form so that each of you will have one. Do this exercise separately. Then compare your responses. Feel free to write down ideas as they come to you in random order. Take seven minutes on each section. Write as fast as you can. Let your ideas flow. All answers are correct. Share and enjoy your responses.

I. What was your notion of the family while you were growing up? What did children do? What did grownups do? What did fathers do? What did mothers do? Who made the decisions? What were the major decisions? How were chores handled? How were the issues of money, anger, family upsets, rituals, religion, etiquette, and meals handled?

_____

_____

_____

_____

II. If you were married before, what was your notion of the family in your first marriage? Respond to the issues listed in the first question.

_____

_____

_____

_____

_____

_____

III.   What is your current perception of the stepfamily?

_____

_____

_____

_____

_____

_____

_____

IV.   How would you like it to be?

_____

_____

_____

_____

_____

_____

_____

_____

_____

_____

Tools for Setting Up Your Family Rules Chart

(Use with Rule 29. Use the Family Rules Chart.)

YOUR FAMILY RULES CHART

Here are your instructions: Use this form simply as a model for your own chart. Add, subtract, and make the rules clear for your family. Remember, all rules should be written in a positive way. (Use *do's,* not *don'ts.)*

School Days	**Weekends and Holidays**
Getting Up	*Getting Up*

- Time _____ (We allow enough time to avoid a.m. chaos.)
- Time _____

- Turn off alarm.
- Make bed.
- Use bathroom.
- Leave sink clean.
- Hang up towels on your rack.

- Turn off alarm.
- Make bed.
- Use bathroom.

Breakfast	*Family Breakfast or Brunch Whenever Possible*

- Eat breakfast.
- Put food back.
- Wash dishes or put them in dishwasher.

- Use sixteen-step model.

_____

Leaving for School

- Leave book bag, sports stuff, gloves, hats, and other things you'll need ready at door.

_____

After School

- Do homework.
- Play. _____
- Do after-school chores.

_____

- Feed animals. _____
- Do personal laundry before adults come home.
- Help to ready things for dinner.
  (Meal preparation chores change each week.)

_____

_____

Planning Activities

_____

Chores

- Clean bedroom _____
- Dust _____
- Vacuum _____
- Water plants _____
- Help with outside work __
- Mow lawn _____

Dinner

Have at least three to four family meals per week.

Use sixteen-step model.

Dinner

Have more family meals per weekend.

Use sixteen-step model— even with take-out

After-Dinner Activities	*After-Dinner Activities*
Homework	Games

Checked by parent for any kids not doing at least *B* work.

_____

Make sure assignment book is accurate

_____

All good grades (*A*'s and *B*'s) get positive rewards.　　Movies

Misrepresentations about papers, projects, and when book reports are due will result in parent assigning similar and additional work.

Projects
Making something, preferably involving a parent teaching a skill.

Homework

Our Bedtime Ritual
(see Rule 32 on Bedtime Ritual)

Our Weekend Bedtime Ritual

_____　　_____

_____　　_____

_____　　_____

About the Stepfamily Foundation

The first organization ever to devote itself to the issues surrounding the stepfamily, The Stepfamily Foundation, Inc. was established in 1975 by Jeannette Lofas, CSW. The Foundation provides memberships, information, short term counseling, and telephone counseling worldwide, as well as training seminars for professionals who wish to become Certified Stepfamily Foundation Counselors.

In 1997, Lofas and her colleagues founded Family 2000, Inc., which conducts research, works with corporations on family issues, and provides speakers around the world.

The Stepfamily Foundation is located at 333 West End Avenue, New York, N.Y. 10023. Call 212-877-3244 for information or visit our website at www.stepfamily.org.